THE CANINE'S CUISINE

A Dive into Dog Food Evolution

by

Heather Olson

Dear Esteemed Reader,

Thank you immensely for choosing this book to join your collection. We imagine that you've already embarked on an exploration of ideas within these pages, and we couldn't be happier about it!

Now, if you find yourself chuckling, pondering, or even debating with the words in front of you, we'd absolutely love to hear about it. If you can spare a few moments to pen down your thoughts in a review, we would be as delighted as a dictionary on a spelling bee!

An Amazon review would be excellent - but hey, we're far from picky. Whether it's a scribble on the back of a grocery list, a tweet, or even a message in a bottle (though that might take a while to reach us), your feedback is gold.

Writing a review might not be as fun as a spontaneous dance-off, but we promise it'll bring grins to our faces, warmth to our hearts, and incredibly valuable insights to future readers.

With Gratitude,

Bo Bennett, PhD
Publisher
Archieboy Holdings, LLC.

Table of Contents

Introduction: Unveiling the Canine Cuisine 1

Unleashing Our Canine Companions............................. 2

Purpose of This Book... 4

**Chapter 1: A Look into the Canine Past:
What Dogs Ate Hundreds of Years Ago**.............................7

Timeline of Ancient Canine Diets................................. 8

Region-Based Diets: What They Ate Where........................ 11

Chapter 2: The Genesis of Commercial Dog Food 16

The Rise and Spread of Packaged Foods 17

**Chapter 3: The Nutritional Needs of Dogs:
An Overview**...24

Understanding Your Canine's Nutritional Requirements......... 25

**Chapter 4: Transitions in Canine Diet:
From Traditional Foods to Kibble**.............................32

Benefits and Drawbacks of the Old Ways 33

Shift to Modern Dog Food 35

Chapter 5: The Inside Story: What Is Actually in Kibble? 39

The Good, the Bad and the Questionable..................... 40

Understanding Labels and Analysis............................. 47

Chapter 6: The Lifespan of Dogs and Their Diets 50

How Diet Influences Lifespan....................................... 50

Common Health Issues Related to Diet 55

Chapter 7: Advertising Tactics of Dog Food Companies 59

Persuasive Strategies and Ploys...................................... 60

Decoding the Marketing Jargon....................................... 65

Chapter 8: The Natural Food Movement:
A Return to Old Ways?...68

Pros and Cons of Raw or Homemade Food 68

Pet Food Regulations, Risks, and Safety 70

Chapter 9: Feeding Your Dog for Health and Longevity 74

Final Thoughts and Recommendations...................................... 74

Resources for Further Exploration 77

Introduction:
Unveiling the Canine Cuisine

Our four-legged friends have been our companions for thousands of years; however, their dietary habits have evolved significantly over time. Today, we find ourselves lost within a world of fancy packaging, complex labels, and endless kibble options. So, it's high time that we turn back the clock and take a deeper look at what our dogs are originally biologically built to feast upon and how their food has changed over time. This book will uncover the mysteries behind the canine cuisine, ensuring that we are well-informed when it comes to understanding what they need for a long, happy, and healthy life.

In the chapters that follow, we'll sketch the timeline of canine diets - from the days when dogs were wild creatures partaking in nature's bounty to now when they're mostly domesticated and heavily reliant on processed foods. We'll go through the genesis of commercial dog food, its rising popularity, and what exactly constitutes the diet that lies within those shiny packets. We'll delve into the nutritional needs of dogs, dissecting what goes into their meals and understanding the role each nutrient plays. This comprehensive overview will enable us to understand our pet's nutritional needs better and make well-informed feeding decisions.

This book isn't limited to the history and nutritional aspects of canine cuisine, but also critiques the current practices. We'll discuss how advertising tactics used by dog food companies often lead us astray. Additionally, the ongoing debate of commercial kibble versus a return to more 'natural' food will be addressed. The ultimate aim is to empower you, the dog owner, to make the best choices for your pet's health and longevity. Be prepared to embark on a journey, one filled with fascinating revelations about our trusted companions' dietary transition over time.

Unleashing Our Canine Companions

The story of dog food begins with the story of dogs themselves. From their ancestral roots as wild predators to their domestication, our canine companions have undergone dramatic changes, not only in their behavior and physical characteristics but also in their dietary needs and preferences. As we delve deeper into the fascinating history of dog food, we understand more about what fuels our canine companions and how best to provide for their unique nutritional needs.

Dogs, like their human counterparts, are creatures of habit. They become accustomed to certain routines, and this includes their meals. A wild dog's diet was composed largely of whatever they could scavenge or hunt. With domestication, however, came alterations in their diet where humans began offering scraps from their meals. This consisted of fruits, vegetables, and meats. With time and the advent of commercialization, these habits have significantly changed.

Feeding our pooches has become an industry worth billions of dollars. It's an industry bustling with different brands, all promising to offer the best nutrition for your pet. But beneath the impressive advertising and vast range of choice, lie some rather murky truths.

For years, we've seen diets for dogs becoming more processed, and convenience seems to triumph over quality. Commercial dog foods, though seemingly convenient and sometimes cost-effective, may not always cater to the nutritional needs of our dogs. A critical look at the evolution of dog food prompts us to pause and consider, are we really serving our canine companions the best diets? Is there a more healthful, more natural alternative to what's become the norm?

While the evolution of dog diets is a topic of interest, it's pertinent that we anchor our conversations on the wellness of our canine companions. Our dogs are more than just pets. They're family. As such, their health and well-being are of paramount importance. From their younger years through to their senior stages, different dogs require different nutrients, and thus, different foods, to thrive.

Among the factors that have influenced the diet of dogs over the years are commercial interests, convenience, and changing human attitudes towards pet care. As the dynamics of our relationship with animals change, it's vital to constantly assess the best ways to ensure their needs are met. Ultimately, the question of the best way to feed our dogs is one that should be informed by science, not just tradition or the latest trends.

To fully comprehend the journey that has brought us to today's canine cuisine, we must delve into the history of dog feeding and understand the transitions and shifts. This journey into the past serves a critical role in shaping our understanding and future decisions concerning the dietary needs of our beloved four-legged friends.

The journey of dog food, much like the journey of dogs from wild beasts to domestic companions, is a compelling story of innovation, industry, and love. From humble beginnings–scraps from the family dinner table–to the rise of a multibillion-dollar global industry, it's a story that continues to evolve alongside our understanding of canine nutrition and health.

It's a story that requires us to ask ourselves, how do we make the best decisions for our pets in a world awash with information, some of it more confusing than helpful? We can begin to answer this question by understanding the link between diet and health, and most importantly, by putting the love we have for our dogs at the forefront of our decision-making process.

Packed conveniently in cans or bags, commercial dog food has undeniably taken over the pet world. But it's worth noting that these products are a relatively recent addition to our pantries. The inception of commercial dog food has affected the dog's diet considerably, altering not just what they eat, but also their health and lifespan.

In the midst of the discussions about dog food, we'll also touch on the influence of advertising strategies used by dog food companies. These methods color our perceptions and drive our buying habits even though they might not always serve the best interests of our pets. Unraveling the truth behind the advertising hype allows us to make better choices for our furry friends.

As we journey together into the heart of canine gastronomy, we'll not only explore the past, but we'll also look ahead. There's been a rising trend of homeowners reverting to the basics, preparing their dog's meals instead of serving kibble. Is this the future of dog feeding? Is it a viable, sustainable option?

In the end, our ultimate goal should be to ensure that our dogs are not just well-fed, but that they're given food that promotes health, vitality, and longevity. Our mission in this book is to steer you in the right direction, revealing the past, examining the present, and gleaning insights into the future of feeding our canine pals.

Unleashing our canine companions is more than just about a walk in the park. It's about embarking on a journey to understand their past and to navigate their future with informed, thoughtful decisions. But it all starts with understanding the story of dog food. Let's turn over the page and begin this exciting adventure.

Purpose of This Book

The primary purpose of this book is multi-faceted: to inform, to educate, to inspire, and to dispel common myths surrounding canine diets. As a dog owner, or as someone contemplating the joys of canine companionship, it is indisputable that understanding what goes into your pet's diet warrants your attention. The wellbeing and longevity of these beloved family members hinge on the quality of the fare we provide them.

The main goal of this book is to uncover the historical narrative that has shaped the making of canine cuisine as we know it today. We aim to examine the journey of canine nourishment over the years, from being domesticated companions of our early ancestors to the commercially fed pets of our modern world.

It's astonishing to thlink of how the diets of our pets have evolved along with our lifestyles and technological advancements. We'll visit the past, tracing the diets of dogs from various regions and looking into how, when, and why the landscapes of dog nutrition began to change.

The foundation of commercial dog food is another key topic we will delve into. The intent here is to enlighten dog owners about the onset of packaged foods, from canned products to the now-ubiquitous dry kibble. Paralleling our fast-paced lives, the convenience of these products cannot be overstated, but what impact has this shift made on the health and lifespan of our canines?

A comprehensive overview of dogs' nutritional needs forms a crucial component of this book's intent. To provide an optimal diet, it is imperative to understand what our canine companions truly need. Proteins, carbs, vitamins, minerals – what should the balance of nutrients be for a healthy, happy pet?

We'll navigate through the controversial terrain of canine food products, specifically kibble – their composition, beneficial and questionable ingredients, and how to interpret food labels. Knowledge is, indeed, power, and the more discerning you are about what's in your pet's bowl, the better equipped you'll be to make informed decisions.

On our journey, we'll also examine the correlations between diet and dogs' health issues, coupled with the impact of various diets on their lifespans. Real-life case studies and research will be integral to this exploration.

This book also aims to unravel the cunning advertising gimmicks employed by dog food companies. Whether it's celebrity endorsements or misleading marketing jargon, we intend to empower dog owners with the ability to see right through these strategies and articulate what's best for their pets.

A light will be shined on the natural food movement, as well. Is there merit in the recent trend of reverting to old ways? What are the pros and cons of homemade or raw food diets? Navigating through the labyrinth of pet food regulations, risks, and safety measures will similarly be important aspects covered in our discussion.

In conclusion, the aim of this book is to serve as an authoritative guide on dog nutrition. It is not intended to recommend specific products, brands, or diets; it seeks instead to provide you with the knowledge and understanding necessary to make the best possible dietary decisions for your canine companion.

Reading this book, we hope you'll come away with a broader outlook on canine nutrition, be more critical of commercial dog food, and confident enough to make dietary modifications in favor of your pet's health and longevity.

Beyond its educative purpose, the book urges dog owners to view the act of feeding their pets with fresh perspective, as an expression of love, a responsibility, and a profound opportunity to invest in their cherished pet's health and happiness.

Remember, when it comes to nutrition, we are each other's keepers—man and man's best friend alike.

Chapter 1:
A Look into the Canine Past: What Dogs Ate Hundreds of Years Ago

As we delve into the past, we find that the diet of our canine companions has greatly evolved along with their domestication. Originally, dogs were akin to their wolf ancestors, consuming a biologically appropriate diet primarily made up of prey, both large and small. Their meals typically consisted of freshly killed animals, and when food was scarce, they'd hone in on carcasses, scavenge for fruits and berries, or delve into insect colonies. As canines began to cohabit with humans, their diet underwent significant changes. Humans began to share their meals with dogs, which shifted the dogs' eating habits from a carnivorous diet to an omnivorous one. This included grains, vegetables, meats, and fish that were part of the human diet, with the specific components varying based on the foods available in the regions where they lived. For instance, in coastal areas, it wouldn't be unusual for dogs to consume a large quantity of fish. On the other hand, in farming communities, their diet would be based more on grains or farm animals. This chapter will provide a comprehensive view into this timeline of the ancient canine diet, aiming to provide a more thorough understanding of the significant dietary changes that have occurred throughout canine history.

Timeline of Ancient Canine Diets

When contemplating the dietary history of canines, it's vital to start at the point of domestication. Early domestic dogs, much like their wolf cousins, were primarily carnivores. Evolution played a crucial role in their dietary shift, as humans began to share their sustenance with dogs.

The timeline begins about 15,000 years ago when evidence of domesticated dogs first emerged. However, some remains discovered suggest domestication could've taken place as early as 33,000 years ago. Early humans likely fed dogs leftovers from hunting expeditions, such as scraps of meat and bones, forming a carnivorous diet in the nascent stages of domestication.

As humans transitioned from nomadic hunters to settled farmers around 10,000 years ago, dog's diets began to change too. As people began to farm and domesticate animals for milk, dogs started receiving scraps of bread, vegetables, and dairy products in addition to meat. This shift formed an omnivorous diet in dogs, demonstrating a crucial evolutionary adaptation.

By 6,500 years ago in China and the Middle East, there are archeological indications showing dogs were given human foods like cereals and vegetables along with meat sources – a telling sign of agriculture's influence on canine feeding habits.

Fast forward to the ancient Roman period, around 2,000 years ago, and dogs were believed to be fed a mix of bread, vegetables, and meat – much like the present diet of dogs. Historical texts also suggest that Roman dogs were sometimes given special meals, a far notion from just leftovers.

In the Middle Ages across Europe, dogs continued to be largely sustained by human scraps. However, during famines and food shortages, dogs often suffered malnutrition due to lack of human surplus. It is also during this era when dogs began to be bred for specific functions like hunting, herding, and guarding, which significantly influenced their diets.

By the 16th and 17th centuries, manuals on dog care started suggesting a variety of foods including bread, milk, and meat. Additionally, some hint towards using medicinal herbs and concoctions indicate an understanding of dietary elements required for the dog's health.

The advent of the Industrial Revolution in the late 18th and 19th centuries brought significant changes to the human world, impacting canine diets too. Industrialization led to the mass production of bread and meat, making these foods more accessible and shaping the dietary habits of dogs and humans alike.

The Victorian era, in the 19th century, was when the role and status of dogs began to significantly transition. Dogs moved from being working animals to cherished pets. With this, their diets also evolved, and specially prepared foods, rather than just scraps, became more commonplace.

However, by the late 19th and early 20th century, a pivotal point in canine dietary history was reached. With increased urbanization and changes in human lifestyle, the tradition of homemade diets started declining, paving a path for the emergence of commercial dog food.

Although canned dog food was patent in the 1860s, it didn't become mainstream until the early 20th century. Following World War II, dry dog food or kibble, due to its convenience and long shelf life, became exceedingly popular.

Today, the vast majority of dogs are sustained on commercial foods. We are now seeing trends of returning to 'traditional' diets that closely mirror what dogs ate before the advent of commercial food. Homemade and raw food diets are becoming popular once again in an attempt to mimic the diet of canine ancestors.

From scraps of meat and bones to dry kibble and canned goodness, the canine diet has undergone remarkable changes over the centuries.

This evolution illustrates the co-dependent relationship that dogs and humans have shared, intertwined in their journey towards development and progress.

Understanding this historical perspective is essential as we consider nutrition for our dogs today. With each piece of kibble, remember that you're not just feeding your pet — you're carrying forward tens of thousands of years of evolutionary history.

In sum, the progression of a dog's diet reflects humanity's own dietary and lifestyle transformations. For better or worse, as dogs became our companions, they've accompanied us at the dinner table too — whether it's sharing spoils from a hunt or a bowl of mass-produced kibble.

From Wolves to Domestic Dogs dives into the fascinating history of how our modern pet dogs have evolved from their wolf ancestors. Our dogs' original ancestors, wolves, lived off the land feasting on small game animals, birds, fish, and even berries and other plant matter when necessary. They had to hunt, scavenge, forage, or even starve – whatever it took to survive in the wild.

Their diet was primarily composed of proteins, fats, and carbohydrates in that order. It wasn't planned or evaluated based on nutritional values but consisted of what was available to them and varied by what they could hunt or scavenge in their respective geographical areas. Their bodies naturally developed systems to handle this raw, unpasteurized, unprocessed diet. As evolution took its course, wolves that were more comfortable around humans had a survival advantage and gradually began to associatively live with us, leading to the first stages of domestication.

Over thousands of years, these increasingly domesticated wolves began to look and behave differently from their wild counterparts. These distinct changes eventually led to the myriad of dog breeds we are familiar with today. But one thing that didn't change as rapidly was their dietary needs. Even as domestic dogs, they were mainly fed scraps of meat, bones, bread, and occasional raw vegetables and fruits from whatever their human companions had on hand, replicating the type of foods they could find in the wild. However, as we progress into modern times, we have seen a pronounced shift in their diet, especially with the advent of commercial dog food. The dogs of today are far removed from their ancient wolf ancestry in lifestyle, but their physiological need for a balanced diet remains consistent.

Region-Based Diets: What They Ate Where

In exploring the historical diets of dogs, it's crucial to acknowledge the variety based on geographical location. Like humans, dogs in different regions ate differently, determined by cultural practices, local climates, and available food sources.

Beginning with Europe, it's important to remember that dogs were used in various roles, such as hunting, farming, and guarding, which affected their diets. Historical records reveal that European dogs' diets predominantly included offal, grains, and vermin as proteins. Dogs were typically fed once a day with leftovers or a special concoction known as "pot liquor", a mixture of meaty bones, vegetables, and barley.

The diets of the dogs in Northern Europe were somewhat different due to the harsh climate. The scarcity of plant foods during winter meant the majority of the dog's diet consisted of fish and other marine animals, along with reindeer and other types of game. It wasn't uncommon to see dogs dining on a seal carcass or chewing on reindeer antlers.

Moving onto North America, indigenous tribes treated dogs not only as companions but also as working animals. Their dietary staples reflected this symbiotic relationship as they enjoyed meat and fish, leftovers from human meals, and occasionally maize or cornmeal. They ate what their human counterparts had, ensuring a diet high in protein and fat while still incorporating essential grain elements.

In the cold Northern areas of North America, dogs led a similar life to their Northern European counterparts. Fetching a substantial amount of their diet from fish, whales, and small mammals. The scarcity of vegetation during the long winter months meant a diet predominantly based on the meat and fat of marine animals.

Heading further South, dogs consumed a diet that was slightly more diverse due to the availability of fruits and vegetables. It was not out of the ordinary to find dogs munching on yams, maize, or lentils along with proteins like fish and poultry.

When we examine Asia's dog diets, there's also a significant amount of variation due to the region's vastness and diversity. Cases from rural areas of Mongolia and Siberia reveal that dogs survived mostly on a diet of sheep and goat offal along with leftovers from their human counterparts. There are also instances of dogs being fed raw horse milk, a common food among the nomadic tribes.

In East Asia, dogs were part of the family and were often given remnants of fish, rice and vegetables, echoing the human diet of the time. As Buddhism spread, owners often strived to lessen the suffering of animals, resulting in diet plans for dogs that emphasized the use of vegetables and less meat.

On a unique note, dogs located on the Indian subcontinent were predominantly foragers, feeding on what was available in human settlements. They consumed a diet of grains, vegetables, and spoiled meat, revealing an adaptive dietary style.

It's essential to stress that, although modern dog food aims to provide balanced nutrition, the diet of canines hundreds of years ago was balanced in an entirely different way. Dogs' digestive systems have evolved to handle a varied and adaptive diet, just like their ancestors did. It's been a survival mechanism perfected over centuries.

Observing and understanding these traditional diets can be extremely informative for contemporary dog owners who strive to provide their dogs with a nutritious and balanced diet. It underlines the importance of variety and balance in a dog's diet, which many commercial dog foods attempt to emulate today.

However, it's important not to romanticize these historic diets. Dogs back then faced many health risks due to dietary deficiencies and exposure to parasites or pathogens, some of which we have now managed to control significantly.

Also, consider that our dogs today aren't working dogs as their ancestors were. They lead more sedentary lives and so may not require a diet as rich in protein or fat. Today's dogs also live longer than their ancestors, thanks to advancements in veterinary care and nutrition. Therefore, it's essential to ensure their diet supports their longevity.

In conclusion, while examining historical canine diets provides us with fascinating insights into how dogs have evolved and adapted, it's crucial to apply these findings judiciously. We must consider modern scientific knowledge about canine nutrition and the specific lifestyle and health considerations for each individual dog.

In Europe, as is the case with various regions of the world, the diet of dogs has evolved significantly over time. Originally, European dogs, just like their wild forebears, thrived on a diet of raw animals - including meat, bones, and organ meats. This was by necessity, as these animals scrounged and hunted for their food, seeking out meals as and when they could.

However, with the advent of domestication and the growth of human societies, these ancient canine diets inevitably changed. Agricultural revolutions introduced new ingredients into the canine diet – animals began to be fed leftovers from human meals as a matter of practicality. These would have included a range of foodstuffs, such as vegetables, fruits, grains and cooked meat. As human civilisations developed, the dogs' diet continued to adapt alongside.

Fast forward to the 18th and 19th centuries, and we see the introduction of bread-based diets for dogs in Europe. The Industrial Revolution saw a dramatic increase in the production and availability of grains which led to an increased use of bread and cereals in the canine diet. European dogs were fed bread soaked in milk or broths made from vegetables or meat as a staple diet. In fact, the term 'dog biscuit' was coined in England in the mid-1800s, marking a significant step towards the commercialisation of dog food that we're familiar with today. However, these diets faced criticism for being heavy in carbohydrates, potentially leading to dental and weight problems, and a shift towards more protein-based diets started to emerge, setting the stage for the next major evolution in dog feeding.

In North America, the past canine diet was heavily influenced by the Native tribes and settlers, each with their own unique methods of food procurement and preservation that were likewise mirrored in the feeding habits of their dogs. Unlike their European counterparts, North American dogs primarily subsisted on a diet closely resembling that of their human partners, consuming the same game animals, fish, grains, and wild fruits. This was largely due to the fact that Native societies saw dogs as part of the tribe; hence, dogs were provided with similar nutrition.

The arrival of European settlers brought changes to the landscape of North American canine cuisine as they introduced new types of animal breeds and plants. Dogs transitioned from a diet high in wild game and foraged food to one that was increasingly domestic, mirroring the shift in human diets. However, geographical variations were still existent. For example, coastal dogs had diets abundant in fish, while those based in farming regions consumed more grains and livestock.

The shift towards commercially available dog food in the late 19th century greatly altered the North American canine diet. The emergence of dog food companies brought about kibbles and canned food that were more convenient and hailed as nutritionally balanced, causing a diminishing reliance on regional food sources and traditional dietary practices. By the mid-20th century, the majority of dogs in

North America were eating a diet primarily composed of commercially manufactured pet food, steering away from their ancestral roving foragers or farming companions' diet.

In Asia, traditional dog diets varied greatly depending on the specific location and period of time. These differences were primarily due to the distinct cultural and agricultural practices across different regions of this vast continent. However, despite these discrepancies, ancient Asian canine diets shared certain common characteristics.

Many areas in Asia, particularly East Asian regions such as China, Japan, and Korea, historically bred dogs both for companionship and consumption. However, dogs kept as pets were not fed the same diet as those bred for food. The former were often given a diet of rice, vegetables, and sometimes fish or small amounts of meat. The latter were fed a more protein-rich diet to increase their body mass. These dog-keeping practices mirror the human dietary habits of the region, where rice and vegetables are staple foods, and protein sources like fish and meat are consumed in smaller quantities.

Further west, in regions like Central Asia where dog breeding was more commonly linked to hunting and herding, dogs were frequently fed a diet rich in raw meat and bones. This diet was closer to that of their wild ancestors and was a reflection of the nomadic lifestyles of these regions where livestock farming was prevalent. It's interesting to note that such practices are making a comeback in certain circles today, with proponents asserting the health benefits of a more natural, raw diet for dogs. Thus, when considering dog food today, it is valuable to remember these ancestral feeding habits that have evolved over hundreds of years, deeply ingrained in specific geographical and cultural contexts.

Chapter 2:
The Genesis of Commercial Dog Food

We've been informed about the various diets of canines throughout different regions and periods in history in the previous chapter. Yet, in the 19th century, a monumental shift took place that significantly altered how we feed our dogs today. As societies became more industrialized, the **commercialization of dog food took off across borders. Enterprising businesses saw a golden opportunity to simplify the feeding process and began selling packaged foods. The first-ever patented dog-food was produced by James Spratt, an electrician from Ohio, who invented a biscuit made of wheat, beetroot, and beef blood after observing dogs devouring hardtack, the ship's biscuit, at the docks. The invention of canned dog food soon followed, primarily composed of horse meat, making it popular during times when the horse population exceeded the need for them as transport. A little later in the last century, dry kibble was introduced. This convenient, non-perishable, and easy-to-store product witnessed a surge in popularity, particularly during World War II due to metal shortages impacting canned food production. This evolution from raw, home-cooked meals to commercial meals has not just changed the texture and components of the food we serve our dogs, but it has also had considerable implications on their health and longevity.**

The Rise and Spread of Packaged Foods

The advent of commercial dog food marked a significant shift in canine nutrition. The rapid urbanization of the 19th and early 20th centuries altered the lifestyles of dogs and their humans alike, precipitating the need for more convenient feeding options. As humans transitioned from subsistence farming to factory and office work, dogs transformed from working animals into beloved family pets.

As we delve into the history of commercial dog food, it's important to note that the packaging industry evolved parallel to the food industry. Industrialization introduced canned goods to people around the mid-19th century. It wasn't until the late 19th century, however, that the resources and technology became available to create food specially formulated for dogs and package it for retail sales.

Englishman James Spratt, an electrician by trade, is generally credited with inventing the first commercially processed dog food. After observing dogs scavenging for leftover biscuits in shipyards, Spratt formulated a biscuit made of wheat meals, vegetables, beetroot, and beef blood. These biscuits, introduced around 1860, were intended for sporting dogs owned by England's upper class.

Seizing the economic opportunity presented by the rising status of dogs within households, other companies soon jumped on the bandwagon. By the early 20th century, it became common for urban dwellers to purchase commercial pet food, leaving behind the days when dogs subsisted on scraps and leftovers.

As we continue our journey through the annals of dog food history, we encounter Ken-L Ration and the introduction of canned dog food in the 1920s. This revolutionary product, primarily consisting of horse meat, gained popularity when horse-drawn vehicles were replaced by automobiles and large numbers of horses became commercially available.

Canned dog food quickly became the preferred choice for pet owners because it was convenient, required no refrigeration, and could be stored for long periods. Despite being more expensive than homemade meals, it was hailed as a complete, balanced diet and enthusiastically endorsed by veterinarians of the time.

However, the landscape of commercial pet food took another sharp turn during World War II when metal rationing impacted the availability of canned food. The packaging industry started manufacturing paper-based bags, making dry food, also known as kibble, the go-to solution for pet owners.

While canned food seemed a significant luxury during the war era, kibble shot to popularity for its convenience, compactness, and extended shelf life. Low costs, bolstered by their use of inexpensive grain and meat byproducts, also played a crucial role in the swift embrace of kibble.

In the subsequent decades, fast-paced advancements in food processing technology facilitated the creation of extruded pet foods, which are essentially kibble that's been cooked under high heat and pressure, expanded and thus made easier to digest. This further accentuated the popularity of kibble among pet owners.

The 1980s marked another significant shift with the emphasis on tailoring diets to different life stages and lifestyles. This era brought forth the creation of various formulas, including puppy food, senior food, weight-control food, and breed-specific food. These advancements allowed for a more personalized approach to dog nutrition that had not previously been possible.

Through a combined effect of convenience, cost-efficiency, and aggressive marketing, commercial dog food has profoundly transformed the landscape of canine feeding routines over the last century. Packaged food's rise and spread have been largely marked by responding to societal needs and technological advances. Yet, it precipitates a new slew of dilemmas and debates over its nutritional adequacy and healthiness, prompting both backlash and reform.

As we deduce from this historical account, one aspect is clear: commercial dog food didn't establish its mark overnight. It was largely driven by societal changes, emerging technologies, economic situations, and evolving perceptions about pet ownership and animal welfare – aspects we'll explore further in the subsequent sections.

Thus, as we delve deeper into the creation and constitution of canned foods and kibble, it's crucial to remember that these developments in the dog food industry were less a sudden revelation and more a gradual evolution, shaped as much by commercial enterprise as by the changing roles of dogs in our society.

The Invention of Canned Dog Food traces back to about the mid-19th century. It was an era marked by rapid industrialization and growth in technology. This led to advances in the production and preservation of food.

The origins of canned dog food are intertwined with the name of an inventive entrepreneur, James Spratt. An electrician by trade, Spratt was born and raised in Cincinnati, Ohio. In the 1860s, while on a sales-related trip to England, he observed stray dogs feasting on hardtack biscuits discarded by sailors. Hardtack, made of flour, water, and sometimes salt, was a dietary staple for sailors during long voyages. Its long shelf-life and resistance to mold made it an ideal food supply. Spratt saw the potential in repurposing a similar biscuit for dogs, aiming to offer a convenient solution for feeding man's best friend.

Back in Cincinnati, Spratt started his dog food business. He put his plan into action and created the first processed dog food, a biscuit made of wheat, beetroot, and beef blood, later known as Spratt's Patent Meat Fibrine Dog Cakes. By 1885, Spratt's creation was popular, with dog owners appreciating the convenience of having a store-bought food for their pets. Spratt's company paved the way for others and established the foundation for the commercial pet food industry.

In the 1920s, a man named Ken-L-Ration launched the first canned dog food in America. Rather than biscuits, this was made of horse meat, a readily available commodity at the time due to an excess of horses. Unfortunately, commercial dog food's reputation took a hit during World War II when metal became a valuable resource for the war effort. It was a common practice to ration metal and, in this regard, canning became less popular. Tin cans were needed for the war, leading to a shift in the commercial dog food industry to create a cost-effective and practical alternative to canned food.

The transition towards more cost-effective manufacturing drove companies to start producing dry dog food in the form of kibble. The ingredients included a mix of meat and grain leftovers encompassing scraps from slaughterhouses and mills that were deemed unfit for human consumption. This new format was less expensive for manufacturers and consumers alike, making it an understandable leap in the world of dog food.

In the following years, dog food recipes became more diverse and started including meals made from specific meat types such as beef, chicken, and fish. The companies also began to integrate vegetables and essential nutrients, aiming to provide a more balanced diet for dogs. Emerging research on animal nutrition played a pivotal role in these developments.

In the 1970s and 1980s, the industry saw another evolution with the introduction of gourmet dog food. This often had fancier ingredients and advertised as superior and advanced nutrition. Many companies also started producing diet-specific foods to cater to the needs of puppies, seniors, dogs with certain allergies, or breeds with specific nutritional needs.

Despite these advances, it's essential for dog owners to remember that while commercial dog foods, including canned options, offer convenience and can meet basic nutritional requirements, they may not always provide the best option for every dog's health. Many commercial diets are still made of lower-quality ingredients and may contain additives, artificial colors, flavors, and preservatives that are not beneficial to a dog's health or may trigger allergic reactions.

It's a good practice to involve your vet in your dog's diet planning, understand the pros and cons of different dog food types, and make an educated decision on what food to feed your beloved pet. Remember, every dog is unique, and what works for one may not work for another. Your dog deserves the best, so it's essential to invest time in understanding nutrition and the history of food options like canned dog food.

The Creation of Dry Kibble traces its origins back to the mid-19th century. Enterprising entrepreneurs observing the rise of packaged foods for human convenience saw an opportunity to do the same for dogs. Before this time, dogs typically ate table scraps or raw meat, a diet closer to what their wild ancestors consumed. Although convenient, this diet wasn't always nutritionally optimal for our domesticated friends. This realization led to the development of dry kibble, designed to provide a balanced diet tailored to dogs' specific needs.

James Spratt, an electrician from Cincinnati, is credited as the pioneer of the commercial dog food industry. On a trip to London in the mid-1850s, he noticed dogs eating discarded, hardtack biscuits, a type of dried bread product used by sailors on long voyages. This observation inspired him to create a nutrient-rich, dry biscuit for dogs, marking the genesis of dry kibble.

After extensive research and experimentation, Spratt launched the first commercial dog food – a bone-shaped biscuit made of wheat, beetroot, and meat. This dog biscuit was easy to store, inexpensive to produce, and had a long shelf life - making it an attractive alternative to table scraps and raw food. The Spratt's Patent Meal Fibrine Dog Cakes won wide recognition and initiated a paradigm shift in how dogs were fed.

However, it took some time for dry kibble to become popular. Until the 1950s, canned dog food was more common, primarily due to its better palatability compared to dry biscuits. But a new processing technique called extrusion marked a turning point in the dog food industry.

The extrusion process, first used by a pet food company named Ralston Purina, involved cooking a mix of ingredients under high pressure and high heat, then forcing it through a die-cut to create the distinctive kibble shapes we know today. After this process, the kibbles were quickly dried to reduce moisture, which significantly extended their shelf life. This innovative technique allowed for a higher volume of production and lower costs, paving the way for dry kibble's widespread acceptance.

Over time, as research deepened our understanding of canine nutrition, the formulations of dry kibbles also evolved. Initial recipes were primarily grain-based, reflecting an understanding of nutrition more suited to humans than carnivorous pets. Nutritional inadequacies, highlighted by health problems in dogs, led to revised formulations that included a greater proportion of meat and a more balanced profile of vitamins and minerals.

Still, cost-effectiveness remained a vital consideration in the manufacture of dry kibble. Some manufacturers began including meat by-products, leftovers from the human meat industry, and even waste products from the grain industry to bring down costs. While these practices helped make pet food affordable for the average pet owner, they also raised questions about the quality of ingredients and the true nutritional value of the products.

By the late 20th century, advances in manufacturing technology, coupled with a growing consumer emphasis on pet health, contributed to rapid diversification in the dry kibble market. Different lines of products emerged, targeting different breeds, ages, sizes, and even specific health conditions.

Today, dry kibble remains a staple of dogs' diet worldwide. The convenience it offers, along with the improvements in formulation and regulation, has bolstered its popularity among dog owners. Despite its humble origins and rocky history marked by questions and controversies, dry kibble continues to be a significant part of our canine companions' lives.

Chapter 3:
The Nutritional Needs of Dogs:
An Overview

The shift in canine diet, from traditional foods to convenient pellets of kibble, presents us with the significant matter at stake—the nutritional needs of our faithful companions. Consider this, each breed of dog carries a unique dietary footprint, hinged on their individual energy levels, size, and overall health conditions. Hence, understanding the nutritional principles for dogs evolves as a non-negotiable facet of responsible pet ownership. Broadly, a dog's diet shimmers with a delicate balance of proteins, carbohydrates, fats, vitamins, and minerals. While proteins arise as the key building blocks of tissues, providing the necessary amino acids for overall growth, carbohydrates shoulder the responsibility of being the primary energy source. Vitamins and minerals, though needed in smaller quantities, cannot be dismissed—even trace amounts can contribute to the biochemical balance inside your pet's body. It's also essential to note that obese and senior dogs may have dietary needs distinct from their youthful or ideally proportioned counterparts. In the following sections, we'll delve deeper into these individual components, discussing their merit, and shedding light on their contribution to your pet's health.

Understanding Your Canine's Nutritional Requirements

Every dog has unique dietary needs that depend on factors such as age, breed, weight, activity level, and overall health. However, an understanding of general canine nutritional requirements is essential to ensure your four-legged friend enjoys optimal health. The primary dietary components vital to your dog's wellbeing include carbohydrates, proteins, fats, vitamins, and minerals. Let's explore each element in depth.

Let's start with carbohydrates, a nutrient group often plagued with mixed reviews in the realm of canine nutrition. Some argue for its necessity, while others believe it's better left out of a dog's diet. The truth is, dogs don't technically need carbohydrates; their bodies can extract the necessary energy from proteins and fats. However, good quality carbohydrates, such as whole grains, provide vitamins, minerals, and fiber that contribute to a well-rounded diet. They also are a valuable energy source that keeps your pooch active and happy.

However, this doesn't mean all carbohydrates are good for your dog. For instance, refined grains and sugars may cause health issues like obesity and diabetes. Therefore, ensuring your dog's carbohydrates come from high-quality sources is vital. Try as much as possible to incorporate whole grains, vegetables, and fruits into your pet's diet.

Moving on to proteins, an essential part of your dog's diet. Dogs, descendants of wolves, are biologically adapted to a primarily carnivorous diet. Proteins supply the required amino acids necessary for healthy tissue and muscle development. In addition, proteins aid in the repair of body cells, the production of essential enzymes and hormones, and bolster immune system function.

Protein requirements can vary greatly based on your canine's life stage and lifestyle. For instance, puppies and lactating mothers need a higher protein intake than adult dogs. Similarly, working dogs or highly active dogs will require more protein than their sedentary counterparts. The source of the protein also matters. A diet rich in high-quality, animal-based proteins (like chicken, beef, or fish) provides more overall nutritional value than plant-based proteins.

Fats, though often given a bad rap, are actually beneficial for your pet. Fats supply the most concentrated source of energy for dogs. They support skin and coat health, cushion vital organs, and also add flavor to food, encouraging the sometimes picky eater. Like with proteins and carbohydrates, the quality and digestibility of the fat are crucial. Animal fats and certain plant oils provide the necessary essential fatty acids dogs require for nutritious diet.

Vitamins and minerals, while needed in smaller quantities than proteins, fats, and carbohydrates, play a vital role in your dog's health. They catalyze biochemical reactions, help maintain the nervous system, aid blood clotting, and keep skin and muscles healthy. Nutritional imbalances can lead to a plethora of health issues, so it's important to ensure your canine is getting a broad spectrum of vitamins and minerals in correct proportions, whether through diet or dietary supplements.

Calcium and phosphorus are minerals that work together to build your dog's bones and teeth, with ratios between the two being particularly important. Other essential minerals include potassium, sodium, chloride, magnesium, sulfur, and trace amounts of iron, zinc, iodine, selenium and copper. Many commercial dog foods use mineral additives to ensure a balanced diet, but always consult your vet if you're unsure.

Vitamins are divided into two groups: fat-soluble (vitamins A, D, E, and K) and water-soluble (vitamin C and B vitamins). Fat-soluble vitamins are stored in the body's fatty tissue and liver, while water-soluble vitamins are not stored and need to be replenished more frequently.

Water, although often discounted as a nutrient, is essential for the life of all animals, including dogs. Water aids digestion, carries nutrients, lubricates joints, and helps regulate body temperature. A dog should always have access to clean, fresh water, as dehydration can lead to serious health problems.

Lastly, fiber isn't technically considered a required nutrient for dogs, but it does provide certain health benefits. Dietary fiber is a type of carbohydrate that aids in digestion by adding bulk and moisture to the dog's stool. This can help keep them regular and alleviate constipation or diarrhea.

Understanding your dog's nutritional needs is a critical first step in promoting their overall health. Whether you're planning to feed your pet a commercially prepared food, or a homemade diet, it's essential that your dog's diet meets all these nutritional requirements. When in doubt, always consider consulting with a knowledgeable vet or a certified pet nutritionist.

Carbohydrates have a complex role in a dog's diet. Unbeknownst to many, carbohydrates are not an essential nutrient for dogs. In fact, their bodies are mainly designed to process proteins and fats. However, that doesn't mean carbohydrates don't have a place in your dog's food bowl. They provide a necessary source of energy and contribute to gut health. Understanding the role and types of carbohydrates crucial for your dog's health is key.

Carbohydrates come in a variety of different forms. Complex carbohydrates like whole grains and vegetables offer a richer source of nutrients than simple carbohydrates such as sugars. They take longer to break down in the dog's system, providing a steadier supply of energy. Muscular and high-energy dogs benefit from complex carbohydrates like sweet potatoes, brown rice and peas which provide sustained energy release. Diet with these carbohydrates ensures the dog doesn't experience peaks and troughs in energy levels which can lead to irritable behavior and poor concentration.

They are also also responsible for fiber, which can help with digestion and nutrient absorption. Fiber is a type of carbohydrate that can't be fully digested by your dog's system. It adds bulk to help move food through the digestive tract and can help manage your dog's weight, as it makes your dog feel full. Fullness equals contentment in dogs, and a hungry dog can be a destructive dog, so fiber plays an important role in the overall contentment and well-being of the dog. Additionally, fiber can help control your dog's blood sugar levels, preventing sudden spikes and dips that can lead to diabetes.

However, they should be provided in moderation. They are not as energy dense as fats or proteins, thus they need to consume more carbohydrates to get the same amount of energy. Consuming too many carbohydrates can lead to obesity and other health problems. Moreover, dogs struggle to digest some types of carbohydrates, due to their shorter digestive tracts. This could lead to upset stomachs and other gastrointestinal issues. So the type and amount of carbohydrates in your dog's diet should be carefully managed.

In conclusion, carbohydrates play various roles in maintaining your dog's overall health - from providing a valuable source of energy, aiding digestion, to even affecting their behavior and mood. A carefully balanced diet containing the right types and amounts of carbohydrates can contribute to your canine friend's overall well-being. Reading labels and understanding the nutritional content in your dog's diet is a responsibility every dog owner should take seriously for the longevity and happiness of their pet.

Proteins play a critical role in your furry friend's diet. This nutrient contributes to the overall well-being of your pet. Unlike humans, dogs require a higher protein intake due to being carnivorous by nature. In the wild, their ancestors thrived on a protein-rich diet, and even though they've evolved and are no longer wolves, this dietary requirement remains.

The first thing to note is that not all proteins are created equal. The quality of protein in the food you feed your dog significantly influences how well they can digest and utilize it. High-quality proteins are derived from animal sources such as poultry, beef, and fish. This is contrary to plant-based proteins such as soy or corn, which aren't as easily, processed by a dog's body because they lack the necessary amino acids that canine requires for optimal health.

Proteins are composed of 22 amino acids, and dogs can produce only half of these in their bodies. The remaining essential amino acids must come from the food they consume. Without adequate protein intake, your dog can become unhealthy, exhibit behavioral changes, and even potentially face life-threatening conditions.

Healthy skin and coats, strong muscles, and good immune function are the visible benefits of an adequate protein intake. However, the internal advantages are equally important. Proteins serve as a vital energy source for dogs, while also promoting cell generation, hormone and enzyme production, and aiding in nutrient transport within the body.

When selecting protein sources for your dog's diet, remember that 'more' doesn't always equate to 'better'. Dogs do need plenty of protein, but what's crucial is balanced nutrition. An excess of proteins can lead to health problems, especially in certain breeds prone to kidney diseases. Therefore, their diet must be carefully formulated to include the perfect balance of high-quality proteins, along with other essential nutrients.

Protein content in commercially available dog food can vary widely. Some foods boast a high 'crude protein' content on their labels, but this doesn't always guarantee its quality or digestibility. Even though the protein content might seem high, it may predominantly be derived from low-quality, indigestible sources. Thus, it becomes essential to understand the nutritional label on the dog food package.

Raw food enthusiasts argue that a carnivorous diet, similar to what their ancestors followed, can provide the optimum protein intake for dogs. However, such diets require careful planning and preparation to ensure they are nutritionally balanced. It's best to consult with a veterinary nutritionist if considering a raw or homemade diet to ensure your dog gets the best quality protein in the right amounts.

The debate over grain-free diets versus traditional kibble also ties into the discussion about proteins. Grain-free diets claim to have higher protein content since they eliminate corn, wheat, and other grains that commonly act as fillers in commercial dog food. However, they often substitute grains with legumes like peas or lentils, which can be problematic due to their lack of certain essential amino acids.

Ultimately, providing your dog with the right type and amount of protein is vital for their health and longevity. It's essential to pick dog food that prioritizes quality of protein sources and provides a balanced diet overall to ensure your pet lives a long, healthy life.

Vitamins and Minerals are an integral part of a dog's diet, just as they are in human nutrition. As we this delve into this aspect, we become aware of the crucial role these elements play in the physiological functions and overall health of our canines. They not only contribute to boosting their immunity, but also aid in skeletal development, nerve functions, and hormone synthesis. A balanced diet with the right amounts of vitamins and minerals ensures dogs' robust health and long lives.

Just like us, our four-legged companions necessitate a variety of vitamins for optimal growth and health. Vitamin A, for instance, plays a vital role in a dog's vision, growth, and immune system. Similarly, B-vitamins like B6 and B12 are essential for their brain function, energy production, and cell metabolism. Likewise, Vitamin D assists in maintaining good bone health, while Vitamin E is well-known for its antioxidant capabilities. Also, Vitamin K is important for the blood clotting process.

Minerals, too, hold considerable significance in dogs' well-being. Elements like calcium and phosphorus are central to their skeletal structure, and potassim helps balance bodily fluids and carry out nerve functions. Iron facilitates oxygen transport in the blood, whereas zinc aids in skin health and wound healing. These minerals, like vitamins, need to be a part of their diet, as dogs are incapable of producing them on their own.

Given the significance of vitamins and minerals, most commercial dog foods are fortified with them. However, not all of these nutrients are always bioavailable for dogs, meaning they may not be fully absorbed by their system. The type of food also matters because cooking processes, such as boiling or roasting, can decrease a food's vitamin content.

While it's crucial to ensure a diet rich in vitamins and minerals, it's equally crucial to provide these in appropriate amounts. An excessive intake can inadvertently lead to hypervitaminosis or mineral toxicity, leading to complications such as kidney failure or calcium deposits in soft tissues. Thus, we need to strike just the right balance - providing all the essential vitamins and minerals without going overboard. It's always recommended to consult a vet or a pet nutritionist to devise a diet plan personalized for your dog's age, weight, and health condition.

Chapter 4:
Transitions in Canine Diet:
From Traditional Foods to Kibble

As we ventured into the heart of the world our canine companions have conquered, we can't help but reflect on the profoundly significant dietary adaptations they've had to endure. It's clear that a dog's banquet table has been dramatically altered from what it once was. A canine's traditional way of eating, as established throughout centuries, was primarily hunting-focused, characterized by a protein-rich diet filled with nature's own raw ingredients. However, the surging pace of modern life brought a paradigm shift to this longstanding culinary practice. While there's a certain elegance to the simplicity of the old ways, steeped as they were in the rhythms of nature, they certainly presented their own unique set of challenges. Predatory existence wasn't always reliable, with food sources often varying according to changing seasons, the controversy of foodborne diseases and the probable burden on the dog owners hunting for food. Balancing these pros and cons catalyzed the inception of commercially manufactured dog food; a shift to a remarkably new era of canine nutrition. Kibble, in particular, emerged as a godsend for canine guardians. It was no flawlessly symmetrical shift, to say the least. The change from traditional foods to kibble was a dramatic one, with humans seeking a solution that would reconcile the need for canine nutrition with the conveniences of modern life. Ironically, this solution carried its own set of benefits and drawbacks. The journey from spartan hunting fare to well-rounded kibble nuggets was fraught with innovation, debate, and a profound desire to do right by our faithful, furry companions.

Benefits and Drawbacks of the Old Ways

Understanding the old ways of feeding canines is important for both appreciating how far we've come and for critically assessing where we stand today. Historically, dogs were fed scraps and leftovers from human meals. This practice held several benefits, one of which was the utilization of otherwise wasted food. No part of an animal hunted by a human was wasted, as anything the humans didn't eat was given to the dogs.

Not only were dogs consuming food that might otherwise have been wasted, but their diet was also varied and often consisted of fresh, whole foods. This included a balance of protein, carbohydrates, and fats that their bodies could utilize for energy, growth, and overall well-being. But even more significantly, they were receiving a wide array of micronutrients from a variety of sources.

Another positive aspect of traditional canine diets was the dental health benefits that came with them. Dogs consuming raw bones and tough meat scraps would naturally clean their teeth during consumption, reducing the buildup of plaque and aiding in the prevention of dental disease.

Historically, dogs also had a closer connection to their food. They would accompany humans on hunts, and their natural behaviors were less restricted. Feeding times were not just about filling their bellies, but also about satisfying psychological needs linked to their wild ancestry.

Despite these benefits, the old ways of feeding dogs weren't without their drawbacks. One primary concern was the inconsistency in nutrition. Even if dogs were getting a range of nutrients from varied sources, there was no guarantee that they were getting all of the necessary nutrients in the appropriate proportions. This could lead to deficiencies or excesses that could adversely affect their health over time.

Another issue was the risk of disease transmission through raw food. A dog being fed raw meat could ingest harmful bacteria or parasites, which could potentially lead to severe illness. This is still a concern today in the raw feeding debate, and many experts caution against raw feeding for this very reason.

While the old ways were resourceful, they weren't necessarily sustainable. With the human population growth, it became increasingly unfeasible to feed dogs in this way. Leftovers and scraps could not sufficiently feed all domestic dogs.

The lack of regulation and standardization was another drawback of the traditional diet. There were no quality controls or standards to follow, and no way to ensure that all dogs were receiving appropriate nutrition. This would eventually lead to the rise of commercial pet foods, which aimed to offer a standardized, balanced diet for all dogs.

A key factor to consider, too, is the lifespan of dogs. In the past, dogs did not typically live as long as they do today. While there's certainly a myriad of reasons for this, one contributing factor may have been diet-related illnesses or deficiencies caused by inconsistency in diet.

While traditional dog diets did have their advantages, ultimately our increasing understanding of canine nutrition, coupled with the practicality issues of feeding a rapidly growing population of domestic dogs, led to the development of commercial dog food.

In the grand scheme, the evolution in canine diet from scraps and leftovers to commercial kibble has its roots in both science and necessity. Though it may lack the romanticism associated with the 'old ways', commercial dog food provided a new and more reliable approach to feeding dogs.

The goal ultimately has been, and remains to be, to ensure our dogs receive a diet that provides all the nutrients they need in the correct proportions, that is safe and free from disease, and that is sustainable and practical in the modern world. As we continue this journey through the evolution of dog food, we will explore how today's dog food measures and addresses these factors.

However, it is also worthwhile to appreciate the lessons we have learned from history, understanding the benefits and drawbacks of the old ways. This comprehension becomes crucial as we explore the present situation of commercial dog food and the emerging trends in canine diets, including a revived interest in raw and natural feeding practices.

In examining the old ways, we learn that ideal nutrition for dogs is not just about meeting their physical needs but also about respecting their natural behaviors and instincts. The future of canine nutrition lies in striking a balance between these factors—honoring our dogs' ancient dietary past while embracing the scientific advancements for their healthier and longer life.

Shift to Modern Dog Food

As we take a step back from traditional dog feeding methods, we come face to face with an evident paradigm shift in the canine diet - the advent of modern dog food. Fueled by the rapid pace of industrialization in the late 19th and early 20th centuries, this shift saw dogs transition from a diet primarily comprising human leftovers and hunted spoils to one dominated by commercially manufactured dog food.

Among the key factors that catalyzed this shift were urbanisation and changes in human lifestyles. As people moved away from farms and into cities which necessitated a fast-paced lifestyle, feeding dogs with scraps or specially prepared meals became less feasible. This paved the way for pet food companies to introduce convenient, ready-to-serve dog food - marking the dawn of the modern dog food era.

Canned dog food was the first type of commercial dog food to make its way into the market. Introduced in the 1920s, it gained the attention of dog owners for its convenience and long shelf-life. While the early versions of canned dog food primarily consisted of horse meat, later variants began to diversify in terms of ingredients and flavours.

However, despite the convenience of canned dog food, its relatively high cost kept it from becoming a staple in every household. Therefore, the quest for an affordable alternative resulted in the creation of dry kibble. Dry kibble, or more commonly referred to as dry dog food, was easy to store, had a longer shelf life, and was easier on the owners' pockets. This revolutionized feeding dogs and quickly became a preferred choice for many.

With the introduction of dry kibble, came the necessity to make dog food nutritious and balanced, providing the dog with all essential nutrients in their required proportions. Consequently, the formulation of dog food became increasingly sophisticated. From the crude beginnings of surplus meat, modern dog food has grown into an elaborate assortment of nutrients, flavors and textures designed to cater to a dog's nutritional needs.

While there's no denying the convenience that commercially manufactured dog food offers, it's also essential to gauge its impact on a dog's overall health and lifespan. On the positive side, most high-quality commercial dog foods are formulated to meet a dog's nutritional needs, making them a balanced and wholesome meal option.

These ready-made foods often incorporate high-quality proteins, carbohydrates, and essential vitamins and minerals to ensure dogs receive all necessary nutrients. Moreover, the consistency in the nutrient levels from bag to bag ensures that the dogs receive a steady diet, less prone to fluctuation or inconsistencies common with homemade meals.

Moreover, commercial dog food also caters conveniently to unique dietary needs. Senior dogs, puppies, and dogs with specific health conditions often need a specialized diet. Commercial dog food companies have a broad range of specially designed, age-specific, breed-specific, and health-specific kibble to cater to these varying needs making the owner's job much easier.

However, it can't be neglected that beneath its shiny exterior, lies contentious issues involving the quality of ingredients, questionable manufacturing practices and confusing marketing gimmicks. With all its benefits, modern dog food has also been a subject of scrutiny and criticism based on the sourcing and safety of its ingredients.

Often, commercial dog foods may include low-quality meat by-products, artificial additives, excessive grains or soy products which may not be best suited for long-term feeding and might lead to a less-than-ideal body condition or health issues. Similarly, manufacturing practices may influence the quality of the final product - safety recalls due to bacterial contamination or the presence of harmful substances are not unheard of in the industry.

Finally, the marketing strategies adopted by dog food companies often add to the confusion in consumers' minds. The lure of branding, the use of terms like 'premium' and 'gourmet', and the adoption of trendy human food fads in dog food disguise the reality behind the labels.

Therefore, while there's no question that modern dog food has revolutionized the way we feed our dogs, pet owners must not shy away from being discerning consumers. By investing time in understanding what's best for their beloved pets, they can ensure that the shift to modern dog food is beneficial and positive.

In our next section, we'll take a detailed look at the reality behind modern dog food - the good, the bad, and the questionable. We'll dissect ingredient lists, unravel food labels and dig deep to provide you with a clearer understanding of what's actually in your dog's kibble and how you can make informed choices.

Chapter 5:
The Inside Story: What Is
Actually in Kibble?

Continuing from our exploration of the transformation in canine diets, we delve into what actually constitutes the kibble that is often a staple in modern dogs' meals. Look at a typical bag of dog kibble, and you might be somewhat perplexed by the list of ingredients. So, what's in it? Well, the first component is often a source of protein - not surprising, given the carnivorous history of our canine companions. This might be named as chicken, beef, lamb, or a variety of other meats, often combined with words like 'meal' or 'by-products'. The more specific the source, the better for your dog. The second major component is usually grains or starchy vegetables to provide carbohydrates, and add bulk. These might be rice, wheat, potatoes, and so on. However, the quality varies significantly, with some brands opting for whole grains and others including less nutritious refined grains or fillers. Then, you have fats for energy, generally from both animal and plant sources, followed by vitamins and minerals, added to ensure nutritional completeness.

But it's not quite as straightforward as this. Kibble also includes less savoury ingredients that could raise eyebrows. Preservatives, for instance, are necessary to keep the dry food from spoiling, but synthetic variants have been linked to health problems. Artificial flavors and colorings, while contributing to the palatability and appearance of kibble, have questionable effects on overall wellbeing.

Food dyes, in particular, have no nutritional value and could potentially contribute to allergies or behavioral issues.

The bottom line is, not all kibble is crafted equal. It is imperative to understand how to decipher labels to differentiate the higher quality products from those banking merely on attractive packaging. We'll delve deeper into this in the next section as we explore pockets of goodness, controversy, and murky areas in the diverse landscape of kibble ingredients. Stay tuned as we dig deeper into the inside story of your furry friend's meal.

The Good, the Bad and the Questionable

In past chapters, we've discussed the transition from traditional food to modern food, which has had a significant impact on our canine companions' diets. Let's now delve deeper into modern dog food, specifically kibble, to analyze what's good, what's bad, and what's questionable about its components.

Kibble has certainly revolutionized the way we feed our dogs. The convenience, long shelf life, and the nutrient-dense components it often boasts make it an appealing choice for busy pet owners. But it's crucial to separate the wheat from the chaff and see what's hidden beneath these attractive labels.

Starting with **the good** part, kibble is typically rich in proteins. Manufacturers usually list specific meat or meat meal as the primary ingredient, signifying a significant presence. These sources provide vital amino acids necessary for the growth, maintenance, and repair of your dog's body. High-quality kibbles also include wholesome grains or legumes as excellent sources of carbs, dietary fibers, and essential micronutrients.

The intended nutritional balance in kibble is another advantage. Unlike raw or homemade diets, commercial dog food follows AAFCO guidelines, ensuring that the food contains the right amount of every nutrient your canine needs. Essential minerals, vitamins, and sometimes even probiotics are also added to support your dog's gastrointestinal health, immunity, and overall wellbeing.

However, everything that glitters isn't gold, and such is the case with kibble. Not all ingredients are beneficial for your furry friend, leading us to **the bad** part. Despite the high protein content claimed by manufacturers, the quality of this protein is often questionable. Some companies use meat from unidentified sources, commonly referred to as "meat by-products" or "animal digest," which can be substandard and hard for your dog to digest.

Fillers, including corn, wheat, and soy, are frequently used to bulk up the food economically. While not intrinsically unhealthy, they are less nutritionally optimal for dogs, providing limited energy and few essential nutrients. Moreover, some dogs may be allergic to certain grains, causing skin issues, digestive problems, or worsened coat condition.

Artificial additives bring us to the darker side of kibble. Preservatives, colorings, and flavorings are often employed to improve shelf life and attractiveness. However, some of these additives might trigger allergies, impair digestion, or even be linked to chronic conditions like cancer.

Now comes the **questionable**. The controversial ingredients in kibble continue to stir debates amongst pet nutrition experts. Although manufacturers maintain each ingredient's safety and usefulness, some elements leave dog owners scratching their heads.

One such ingredient is animal by-products. Depending on the source, these by-products can range from highly nutritious (like organ meat) to potentially harmful. The vague term leaves pet owners in the dark about what they are really feeding their dogs.

Pea protein, lentils, or potatoes are another group of controversial foods. Often used as a meat substitute, these so-called novel ingredients have been associated with dilated cardiomyopathy (DCM) in dogs.

Yet, manufacturers argue that the issue is more complex and not solely connected to these ingredients.

The debate about grain-free diets is another head-scratcher. While some argue that dogs are omnivores and benefit from grains, others believe that dogs are primarily carnivores and grains are an unnatural addition to their diets that cause allergies and digestive issues.

With all these potential landmines, understanding labels and nutritional analysis becomes even more critical for pet owners. The next sections will guide you through discerning the good, the bad, and the dubious elements on your dog's kibble label.

In conclusion, while kibble can be an excellent, convenient way of feeding your dog, it's essential to understand the ingredients to make the best choices. Remember, a well-balanced diet is about quality, not just quantity, so opting for high-quality kibble can mean all the difference in your beloved pet's health and longevity.

Beneficial Ingredients Understanding what makes up a healthful and wholesome diet for your dogs is crucial to ensuring their nutritional needs are met and they live a vibrant, healthy life. There is a myriad of beneficial ingredients that are good for their health, including different types of proteins, certain carbohydrates, a host of vitamins and minerals, and essential fatty acids. So let's delve into what each category holds and why they're immensely munificent for your furry friends.

Protein stands as the pillar of your dog's diet and should invariably constitute the primary ingredient. It's quintessential for growth, maintenance of a healthy body, and adequate energy. Your dog's food should ideally contain proteins from whole sources like beef, chicken, fish, or lamb. Apart from this, organ meats like liver and kidneys can also offer a richness of nutrients that can considerably boost your dog's health.

Carbohydrates provide your dogs with the energy they need to run, play and keep their tails wagging. However, it's essential to choose the right kind of carbohydrates, such as potatoes, rice, quinoa, oats, or vegetables. These are easier to digest and have plenty of other nutritional benefits that are superior to fillers like corn or wheat.

When we talk about beneficial ingredients, we can't possibly overlook the colossal role that vitamins and minerals play for our canine friends. Magnesium helps in nutrient absorption and nerve function. Calcium, phosphorus, and Vitamin D contribute to a healthy skeletal system. Antioxidants like Vitamin A and E enhance the immune system and help maintain your pup's youthful vigor.

Vitamin B is essential for your dog's metabolism and supports healthy growth and development, whereas Vitamin K plays a crucial role in the blood clotting process and wound healing. Notably, an array of minerals such as zinc, copper, iron, and selenium are significant for metabolic function, red blood cell production, and they support a meritorious immune system as well.

Fats, often regarded with misguided apprehension, are fundamentally essential for your dog's health. They're the primary source of energy for dogs and are integral for keeping the skin and fur healthy, reducing inflammation, and achieving overall well-being. Look for foods containing Omega-3 and Omega-6 fatty acids, found richly in fish oils and flaxseed.

Fiber, though not a necessity for dogs, serves a multitude of health benefits that make it a shining star in your pet's diet. It aids in maintaining a healthy weight, can regulate blood sugar levels, and fosters colon health. A diet rich in fruits, vegetables, and whole grains will ensure your dog gets an ample amount of fiber.

The inclusion of probiotics and prebiotics in your dog's diet can augment their digestion and boost the immune system. These are usually found in foods that have been fermented like yogurt or can be added to your dog's regular diet in supplement form.

Many commercial dog foods contain added bonuses like glucosamine and chondroitin, which are beneficial for maintaining healthy joints, particularly in large breed dogs, senior pets, or those with active lifestyles. Similarly, foods fortified with lutein can strengthen your four-legged friend's eyesight and heart.

As a responsible pet parent, you're the custodian of your dog's health, and the foods you choose to feed your pet can significantly impact their longevity and vitality. Understanding the impact of these beneficial ingredients can help you make informed choices about your dog's diet, ensuring they receive all the necessary nutrients for a hale and hearty life.

Controversial Ingredients Nowadays, it might come as a shock to realize that the neatly packaged kibble we routinely feed our dogs every day may not always contain the best ingredients. In fact, the world of commercial dog food has seen its fair share of controversial ingredients mixed in with the myriad of components used to create these meals for canines. All things considered, let's dive in and explore some of the most contentious ingredients popping up in dog food, scrutinize their potential effects on health, and help you become more knowledgeable when choosing your pet's diet.

Believe it or not there are by-products derived from the rendering process that wolf down unwanted parts of meat that are regarded as unfit for human consumption. This includes processing the remains of animals after the prime cuts and innards have been removed. Commonly known as meat by-products or meat meal, it's a product that is highly debatable. Some argue that it provides a dense source of animal protein and reflects a dog's natural diet. Conversely, critics point out that these by-products often come from questionable sources and can contain low-quality tissues.

Next on the list is corn, one of the many grain products found in numerous dog foods. While there's nothing harmful about corn per se, it's not exactly the most nutritious item for a carnivorous animal. The nutritional content of corn is debated because it's hard for dogs to digest and some may be allergic to it. Worst yet, cheap, non-nutritive filler grains such as this one are often used in lower-end kibbles to bulk up the product, which contributes very little to a balanced diet.

Then we have soy, which is a bone of contention due to its estrogen-like compounds that can potentially meddle with a dog's hormonal balance. Yes, it does provide a source of protein, but they are plant proteins that are less digestible and less nutritious for dogs than animal proteins. Furthermore, allergic reactions to soy are not uncommon among dogs.

Added sugars, another contentious component, are primarily included to make the product more palatable for our furry companions. However, sugar essentially offers no nutritional benefits while contributing to obesity and dental issues. Therefore, it's more of a wolf in sheep's clothing. It can appear on labels as beet pulp sugar, glucose, sucrose, or dextrose.

Artificial colours, while not inherently hazardous, have also become a topic of consternation. They are only included to make the food more attractive to the human owners. It's safe to say that your mutt couldn't care less about the colour of its food. Moreover, there are concerns that some artificial colours are linked to different health problems, including hypersensitivity reactions.

Another ingredient that could potentially affect your fur friend's health is propylene glycol. This, frighteningly, is a component of antifreeze, used in dog food as a stabilizer and to keep it moist. Although it's generally deemed safe, it can become toxic in large amounts. It has been banned in cat food due to this risk but is still present in many canine diets.

Next, there are preservatives. While some are benign and natural, others have sparked controversy. Two such widely used preservatives are butylated hydroxyanisole (BHA) and butylated hydroxytoluene (BHT). Both are effective at preserving fats in pet food, increasing shelf life. Unfortunately, both BHA and BHT have been flagged as potential carcinogens by various health organizations.

Let's not forget about salt either. Just like humans, dogs, too need some sodium in their diets. However, the dispute arises when salt is added to dog food in excess. Too much salt is unhealthy for dogs and may contribute to high blood pressure and increased thirst, and could potentially lead to kidney and heart disease.

Xylitol, often found in peanut butter, certain sweets, and other processed foods, is a major debate starter among pet owners. While this sweetener is safe for humans, it is highly toxic to dogs. It leads to a rapid insulin release, causing hypoglycemia (low blood sugar) and can even result in liver failure. Therefore, dog owners are advised to check labels rigorously, especially when giving human foods to their pets.

Lastly, the mystery that is usually listed as "animal digest" rounds up our list of controversial ingredients. Despite its innocuous name, animal digest is a concentrated soup that can contain various rendered (cooked down) parts of animals. The ambiguity of the term leaves room for the inclusion of less desirable and potentially harmful substances.

Awareness is the key here. As pet owners, it's our responsibility to understand what exactly we are putting in our pet's dish. The food we provide forms the basis for their overall health and longevity, and as such, knowledge of these controversial ingredients can be a potent tool.

Knowing the potentially harmful ingredients lurking in the dog food aisle allows us to make an informed choice, considering our dogs' health and vital nutritional needs. Not all ingredients are equally beneficial, and some pose significant health risks, despite being commonly used.

We must bear in mind that every dog has its unique nutritional needs influenced by factors such as age, breed, weight, and health status. It's always paramount to consult with a veterinarian before making major changes to your pup's diet or if you have concerns about your pet's food.

In conclusion, the controversial ingredients in dog food range from harmless yet unnecessary additions such as artificial colours, to potentially detrimental ones like propylene glycol or too much salt. It's important to consider these factors when choosing a nutritious, balanced, and safe diet for our dogs.

Understanding Labels and Analysis

Understanding the labels and analysis on your dog's kibble package can be like reading a different language. However, it's critical to comprehend this information for the sake of your dog's health and well-being. At first glance, the phrases on the package may seem overwhelming, but let's break it down.

Firstly, 'guaranteed analysis' is a common term you'll encounter on dog food packaging. This analysis is primarily to provide nutritional percentages for minimum crude protein, minimum crude fat, maximum crude fiber, and maximum moisture. Note that the term 'crude' denotes the method of testing the ingredient, not its quality.

These figures might seem straightforward: higher protein and fat, lower fiber and moisture, right? It's actually more complex than that. The moisture content, for example, affects the percentages of other nutrients. Dry foods typically contain less moisture than wet food; therefore, to make an accurate comparison between the two, you'll need to take the moisture into account.

Another crucial aspect to understand on dog food labels are the ingredients. They're listed in order of weight, from highest to lowest. The first few ingredients are of utmost importance as they make up the majority of the content. Keep an eye out for specific types of meat listed as the first ingredient, such as chicken or beef, rather than vague terminologies like 'meat' or 'poultry'.

Many dog food packs play fast and loose with their ingredient names. For instance, 'chicken meal' sounds more appealing than 'chicken by-product meal', but it's not necessarily better. The term 'meal' indicates that the ingredient has been rendered or cooked down to a concentrated protein powder. While 'by-product meals' do contain organs that are rich in nutrients, 'meat meal' indicates higher-quality cuts. Consequently, neither is inherently bad. It all comes down to sourcing and processing, which is information you might not find on the label.

Another tricky term to look out for is 'flavor'. Foods labeled as a specific 'flavor' need not contain any significant amount of that ingredient. So, 'beef flavor' kibble might have little to no actual beef, and the flavor can come from beef meal or even artificial flavorings.

Also on the label, you'll find phrases like 'complete and balanced'. You'd expect that this means the diet contains all the requisite nutrients for your dog. This is indeed the intended implication, but the standards to call a diet 'complete and balanced' are quite broad. It means the food meets minimum standards for key nutrients, but whether these minimums and maximums are ideal for your specific dog's health and life stage isn't guaranteed.

Speaking of life stages, dog food labels usually indicate whether the product is intended for puppies, adult dogs, or senior dogs. Some kibble is labeled 'for all life stages', which means it's formatted to meet the most stringent of the three stages. Keep in mind though that just because a food meets these requirements, does not mean it would be the best for all dogs or all life stages.

Where a product is made can also have a significant impact on its quality. For example, 'made in the USA' doesn't necessarily mean that all the ingredients were sourced from the USA. It's also important to note that while the US has stricter pet food regulations than some countries, dangerous recalls have occurred with American-made foods too, often due to problems with the ingredients sourced overseas.

Lastly, some labels will boast a statement about 'no preservatives, artificial colors, or flavors'. While this might sound like a positive, it often isn't saying much. Many dog foods use natural preservatives, which can be a good thing, and colors and flavors aren't significant contributors to nutrition, so their presence or absence isn't a strong marker of a food's overall quality.

While it may feel like a crash course in pet food nutrition, grasping the true meaning behind label claims is a necessary part of responsible dog ownership. As we continue to delve into the complex world of canine nutrition, keep in mind that a well-informed owner makes the best choices for their pooch's health and wellness.

So, next time you grab that bag of kibble off the shelf, take a moment to parse the label. Knowledge is power, and understanding what's actually in your dog's bowl can greatly impact his longevity and quality of life.

Chapter 6:
The Lifespan of Dogs and Their Diets

Continuing from our exploration of kibble content, it's crucial to discuss how diet impacts a dog's lifespan. Time and again, scientific studies have shown an intense correlation between diet and longevity in canines. Take the detailed research conducted on Labrador retrievers, for example, where some were fed a restricted-calorie diet. The results overwhelmingly indicated that those Labs on the calorie-controlled diet lived significantly longer than their unrestricted counterparts. It's not only about extending age, though. Dogs that follow a balanced diet can sidestep many common health complications such as obesity, dental disease, and even certain types of cancer. The quality of food plays directly into how the body performs, after all. Therefore, appropriate nutrition fuels not just any life, but a quality one. Our furry friends' energetic frolic in the park, or those bright eyes that greet you each morning, can, in part, be attributed to the food they consume. As we dive into this chapter, we'll explore specific health issues related to diet and further examine the crucial role of diet in enhancing the lifespan of our dogs.

How Diet Influences Lifespan

Diet plays a pivotal role in the lifespan of dogs. Throughout the evolution of canines, from wild wolves to domesticated dogs, their diets have evolved drastically. The changes are not just about the nature of the food, but also about how it's prepared. While natural raw diets can enhance vitality and longevity, low-quality commercial diets can sometimes shorten lifespan and cause health problems.

Quality is an essential facet of diet. For instance, the quality of protein in a dog's meal is significantly more critical than the quantity. Protein from high-quality sources like meat and fish provides all the essential nutrients for dogs, contributing to overall health and longevity. Conversely, animal by-products, often used in low-cost options, don't meet the same nutritional standards.

Another massive influence on a dog's lifespan is the type of food they consume, such as dry, wet, raw, or homemade diets. Dry dog food, the most commonly fed type, is often severely heat-treated, which can destroy its nutritional content. Wet food avoids this issue, but it may be high in salt, artificial colors, and preservatives, all of which can negatively impact lifespan.

A raw diet, as nature intended, can maximize nutrient availability. Raw food is rich in enzymes and probiotics, promoting healthy digestion, shiny fur, and overall vitality. However, if not done right, raw food can also lead to nutritional imbalances and potential bacterial contamination, posing health risks.

With regards to homemade meals, it provides dog owners full control over their canine's diet but demands careful planning and preparation to offer balanced nutrition. If done right, homemade food can help maintain a dog's weight, keep their coat shiny and their skin healthy, all of which aids longevity.

Portion control and obesity also directly impact a dog's lifespan. Canine obesity is a growing issue and can lead to numerous health problems including diabetes, heart disease, and joint problems, hence reducing their lifespan.

On the other hand, fatty acids, particularly Omega-3s found in fish oils and certain seeds, provide exceptional benefits, including promoting healthy skin and coat, improving cognitive function in older dogs and aiding in weight control. Such nutrient-rich diets, combined with protein sources, can help dogs live longer, healthier lives.

Feeding your dog a biologically appropriate diet can potentially reduce the risk of some chronic diseases. A well-balanced diet can help maintain your dog's immune system, helping him fight off illnesses and infections more effectively, thereby prolonging his lifespan.

When selecting food, being aware of possible allergies and intolerances your dog may have is essential. Just like humans, dogs can have food allergies that can impact their lifespan. Consuming foods or ingredients that a dog is allergic to can result in inflammation, an increase in auto-immune diseases, and a decreased quality of life.

Additionally, dogs often have a lower biological tolerance for certain foods, like grapes, raisins, chocolate, and sugar substitutes like xylitol, which are toxic to canines and can cause serious health problems or even death.

Insuring a well-balanced diet enriched with necessary vitamins and minerals for dogs such as Vitamins A, D, B complex, and more, as well as minerals like calcium and phosphate, is another considerable factor that directly impacts a dog's life expectancy.

Vitamins and minerals help various bodily functions, such as maintaining a shiny coat, keeping bones strong, and maintaining overall health. Any deficiency in these vitamins and minerals can lead to health issues which might shorten their lifespan.

In conclusion, feeding your dog a balanced and nutritious diet is one of the most effective ways to improve its lifespan. In essence, a quality diet can help your beloved pet live a longer, healthier life.

The importance of a healthy diet cannot be understated, therefore becoming an educated dog owner with a solid knowledge of canine nutrition is essential to extend the lifespan of your pet. After all, our dogs rely on us to ensure they live the best life possible.

The bottom line is that our dog's diet can spell the difference between a life fraught with health problems and a long, healthy life filled with vitality and wellbeing.

Case Studies and Research As we delve into the connection between the diets of dogs and their lifespan, numerous case studies and a vast array of research materials heavily influence our understanding. Science often plays a pivotal role in shaping our perspectives, and in the realm of canine nutrition, it has a spotlight.

For instance, a 2005 study carried out in the United Kingdom highlighted the difference between the lifespans of dogs fed homemade diets and those fed commercial kibble. The results demonstrated that canines with homemade meals had an average lifespan of 13 years, while those fed commercial food averaged around ten years. This research reveals the stark contrast and makes a bold statement about the impact of diet on a dog's lifespan.

Further studies have specifically peered into the effects of specific ingredients found in various dog foods. A research article published in the Journal of Animal Physiology and Animal Nutrition in 2007 pointed out how animal by-products, often used in kibble, contribute significantly to the development of health problems like obesity, kidney disease, and cancer. The study served as a wake-up call, showcasing not just what dogs are eating, but also what these ingredients might be doing to their bodies.

Another prominent study that has shone light on canine lifespan and diet is a 2002 study performed by the University of Pennsylvania School of Veterinary Medicine. The research compared comprehensive blood work from dogs who were fed a raw, meat-based diet with those fed a diet of commercial pet food. Dogs on the raw diet had lower mean values in multiple important health markers, such as cholesterol levels, raising the question of how our dogs' diets might be affecting their health at a biochemical level.

Audacious findings came from a 2013 study by Purdue University, which shed light on the role of water in canned dog food. The study found that canned food, which typically has a high water content, was linked to a significantly reduced risk of bloat—a dangerous condition for many breeds. This highlighted yet another angle to consider: the texture and constituents of the food beyond the basic nutritional content.

Additional research has explored more specific dietary needs of various breeds. For example, no two dog breeds are created equally, at least, not in terms of their diet. Boxers, for example, are known to have sensitive stomachs and can benefit from a highly specialized diet as evidenced in a study published in the Journal of Veterinary Internal Medicine in 2004. This research emphasized breed-specific dietary needs, further complicating the quest towards universally optimal nutritional guidelines.

Another eye-opening thing that research has probed into is the issue of food allergies in dogs. An enlightening study from the University of Helsinki in 2017 discovered that certain protein sources are more likely to cause allergies in dogs, making the protein content choice in dog food crucial for avoiding allergenic responses.

Research into the effects of additives in dog food has also elucidated potential harms. A study in 2017 by The Royal Veterinary College in London indicated that some pet food additives, especially certain coloring agents, could be linked to behavioral issues in dogs.

And lest we forget, there's the pivotal ongoing study by The Dog Aging Project, spanning from 2018 to the present, which investigates how genetics, environment, and diet among other factors, impact canine lifespan and health. The output from The Dog Aging Project is undoubtedly setting new benchmarks in understanding dog lifespan and diets.

Of course, even within these case studies and research, there exists a wide range of debate and countering viewpoints. There are always additional factors to take into account including a dog's individual genetic makeup, overall health, and activity level. As such, while the science can guide us, it's essential to keep the big picture in mind.

Looking forward, it is imperative to continue researching and conducting case studies to further understand the intricate relationship between canine diets and their health outcomes. With the rise in technologies and research methods, information is now readily accessible more than ever, paving the way for a future with healthier, longer-living dogs.

These studies provide a foundation of knowledge but should not be the sole benchmarks in making decisions about your dog's diet. Instead, they simply add another tool for dog owners to make informed choices about what is best for their canine companion. As always, dog owners should engage with their vet to determine the dietary routine that will best serve their dog's health and longevity.

To sum up, the connection between a dog's diet and longevity is not a simple narrative. An array of variables come into play, as illuminated by these studies. We must bear in mind, though, that science is a continually evolving field, and what we understand today may not hold tomorrow. So, let's keep our minds open, keep questioning, and, above all, prioritize the wellbeing of our furry friends.

Common Health Issues Related to Diet

As we consider the lifespan of our canine companions, understanding the potential health issues related to their diet is crucial. Our dogs' health is significantly influenced by their nutrition, just as it is in humans. Let's delve into some common health problems faced by dogs primarily due to poor dietary habits.

The first common ailment observed in dogs with poor diets is obesity. As in humans, excess weight in dogs can lead to a host of other health problems. Obesity in dogs is usually the result of high calorie intake and inadequate exercise. Feeding your dogs calorie-dense commercial diets without accounting for their actual energy needs can cause obesity.

The repercussions of obesity in dogs are manifold. It puts them at an elevated risk for serious conditions such as insulin resistance and type 2 diabetes, heart disease, osteoarthritis, and certain types of cancer. A stepped-up exercise routine complemented with a carefully regulated diet plan can effectively combat this condition.

Dental diseases also find their roots in poor nutrition. Ignoring dental health can lead to periodontal diseases that provoke inflammation and tooth loss in dogs. A diet rich in carbohydrates, especially simple sugars, provides nourishment to harmful bacteria, causing an increase in dental plaque.

Hereditary factors can make some dogs more susceptible to dental diseases compared to others. However, a carefully chosen diet, including dental chews and specially formulated foods, can manage and sometimes even reverse such conditions.

Just like humans, dogs can also suffer from food allergies, and these are often linked to particular dietary proteins. Prolonged exposure to these proteins may trigger a response from the dog's immune system leading to symptoms like itchiness, skin infections, and gastrointestinal issues. Identifying and eliminating the allergen from the diet is the best way to tackle food allergies.

Substandard diets are also prime culprit behind skin disorders in dogs. Insufficient intake of essential fatty acids, notably Omega 3 and Omega 6, can lead to dry and itchy skin. Prioritizing a diet balanced in fatty acids can help maintain healthy skin and a shiny coat for your dog.

Pancreatitis, an inflammation of the pancreas, is another health issue that can be triggered by a high-fat diet. Overfeeding, especially foods high in fat, can lead to this painful condition. Dogs with pancreatitis require a low fat, moderate protein, and highly digestible diet to manage their symptoms effectively.

Joint issues, such as arthritis, can take root in a dog's body due to an imbalanced diet. Lack of essential nutrients such as glucosamine, chondroitin, and omega fatty acids can cause degradation of the joint health in dogs. Overweight dogs are particularly prone to arthritis as excess weight puts pressure on their joints.

They can also suffer from metabolic disorders like Hypothyroidism that slows their metabolism causing weight gain, lethargy, and skin issues. Proper diet coupled with medication can manage hypothyroidism effectively.

Bladder stones in dogs are often a result of a specific diet that allows minerals to crystallize in the urine, forming stones. The composition of these stones often reflects the types of minerals in excess in a dog's diet. It's often controlled with a specifically formulated diet that prevents the formation of crystals.

Preserving brain health as a dog ages is another area where diet plays a critical role. The right diet rich in antioxidants and a specific kind of fat, known as medium-chain triglycerides, can maintain and protect a dog's cognitive functions.

When it comes to dog health issues related to diet, prevention is always better than cure. Opting for a balanced, age-appropriate diet for your dog, along with regular exercise, can keep most of these health challenges at bay. Observing your dog's health changes and discussing them with a veterinarian can lead to early detection and simpler resolutions to dietary health issues.

In conclusion, a proper diet isn't just about keeping your dog's tummy full. It's about feeding them the right nutrients in appropriate quantities to maintain their overall health and prolong their lifespan. Always remember, every dog is unique and might need a customized nutritional plan that caters to its breed, size, age, and overall health.

Armed with this knowledge, we can all better prepare ourselves to give our furry friends the longest, healthiest lives possible.

58

Chapter 7:
Advertising Tactics of Dog
Food Companies

Having recognized the complex interplay between diet, health, and longevity in dogs, for Chapter 7 we turn our attention to the less transparent world of advertising employed by dog food companies. Persuasive strategies and ploys are rife in this highly competitive sector. Endorsements by dog-loving celebrities attempt to individualize brands and connect with consumers on a personal level, while emotive appeals endeavor to evoke feelings of guilt, compassion, or even fear to drive consumers to their products. These strategies fundamentally rely on the bond between owners and their dogs. At the same time, projected images of frolicking puppies, glossy coats, sparkling eyes, and satisfied wagging tails target an emotional response, leaving us convinced that this dog food is surely the key to a happy and healthy life for our beloved pets. However, one must learn to look past the enticing visuals and charming narratives to understand the real substance behind the marketing jargon. Words like "holistic", "premium", "natural" and "artisan" are often thrown around liberally, but may bear little coherence to the actual nutritional value of the product. As owners desiring the best for our dogs, it's vital to dissect these messages and accurately assess the truly beneficial offerings versus artful, but potentially misleading, marketing.

Persuasive Strategies and Ploys

Delving into the myriad of techniques dog food companies utilize to promote their products, persuasive strategies play a central role in the success of these endeavors. From emotionally charged advertisements to deploying celebrity figures for product endorsements, an intricate web of persuasion is crafted with precision and finesse, all aimed at capturing the consumer's attention, stirring their emotions, and ultimately influencing their purchasing decisions.

One commonplace persuasion method is the narrative built around the concept of providing optimal nutrition for pets. All dog owners want their canine companions to live long, healthy lives, and dog food companies often capitalize on this sentiment. The tactics employed range from explicitly stating health benefits of a particular diet to the clever positioning of nutritional buzzwords like "natural", "grain-free" or "holistic". Of course, not all advertised claims stand up to scrutiny, underscoring the importance of making informed, critical decisions when it comes to feeding your furry friends.

Product packaging also plays a pivotal role in the marketing sprawl. Bright, attractive colors and images of happy, active dogs are intentionally chosen to catch your eye and create an optimistic image about the product. More often than not, these packaging designs feature pastoral scenes or robust canines in peak physical condition, subtly hinting at a promise that their product is a gateway to achieving this ideal.

Furthermore, dog food companies have a knack for presenting complex scientific data in simplified ways. Graphs, diagrams, and statistics are often used on packaging or promotional platforms to lend credibility to their nutritional claims. The problem comes in when this scientific evidence is cherry-picked, potentially leading consumers to conclusions that don't tell the full nutritional story.

The use of emotional appeals is another potent strategy applied by dog food companies. Heartwarming advertisements showcasing strong bonds between dogs and their owners play to the feelings of consumers. Key phrases such as "show them you care", "because they're family", or "give them the best" can strike a chord, enticing dog owners to believe that purchasing that particular product is a demonstration of love for their pets.

A ploy that's seen a substantial rise in popularity is the deployment of celebrity voices or faces in advertisements. By associating their product with a known public figure, companies hope to leverage the celebrity's place in pop culture to attract customers. It instills a sense of trust and familiarity in the consumer's mind, making the product seem more appealing.

The marketing cogwheels are also driven by companies touting specific formulas for different dog categories. Products are differentiated by size, age, breed, or dietary need, encouraging pet parents to purchase specialty foods over generic ones. While there's some merit in catering to individual dog needs, the extent of specific tailoring varies from brand to brand and should be carefully evaluated.

Directly addressing the dog consumer is another appealing tactic that often captures dog owners' attention. Phrases such as "your dog will love it" or "your furry friend won't be able to resist" aim to establish a connection between the product and the pet, further motivating dog owners towards a purchase.

Testimonials and reviews are also a classic marketing strategy. Positive reviews and endorsements can build consumer trust and create momentum around a product. However, it's essential to remember that individual pet experiences can differ, and a product that worked wonders for one dog might not have the same effect on another.

Eco-conscious branding has also begun to influence dog food marketing. With rising awareness about environmental concerns, brands offering eco-friendly or sustainable products have gained momentum. Some companies advertise plant-based diets, reduced packaging, or sourcing from ethical suppliers as part of their brand identity.

Finally, it's crucial to remember that discounts, sales, and loyalty programs are also formidable elements in the arsenal of persuasive strategies. Resulting in immediate savings, these tactics can often sway consumers' decisions towards certain products or brands.

Keeping all these strategies in mind, it's essential to understand that these are all geared towards driving sales, and not all claims may be entirely accurate. Dog food companies, after all, are businesses with profit at their core. It's up to pet parents to arm themselves with accurate information and carefully scrutinize what goes into their pet's food bowl. Ultimately, our goal is to ensure that our four-legged friends are fed diets that optimize their health and longevity.

Celebrity Endorsements have become a pervasive advertising strategy used by mainstream dog food manufacturers to sway consumers. As we've discussed the progression of dog food from its basic origins to the commercial juggernaut it is today, it's important to take note of the marketing techniques used to promote these products. One of the most noticeable tactics is the use of famous personalities to endorse the products.

The use of celebrities in advertising is not a new strategy. It's been a proven method to capture attention, build trust, and ultimately persuade consumers to buy products. The rationale is simple, yet effective: we often admire and aspire to be like our favorite celebrities. As such, we're likely to emulate them, even down to the type of food we feed our dogs.

High-profile figures like Rachael Ray, who launched her own line of 'premium' dog food, or Ellen DeGeneres, co-owner of Halo, Purely for Pets, provide a sense of credibility and quality to the brands they're associated with. Not forgetting Cesar Millan, the globally recognized dog behaviorist, who has his own line of dog products including food.

While their fame can certainly make a brand more visible, it's important to understand that this does not necessarily equate to nutritional quality. A famous face on a can of dog food is no assurance that the food is the best choice for your pet. Though these endorsements may seem honest and well-intentioned, the ultimate goal of any business is to sell a product.

Furthermore, many celebrities likely do not have comprehensive nutritional or veterinary knowledge. While they may indeed care deeply for animals, that doesn't mean they are qualified to guarantee the nutritional adequacy of a dog food product. Therefore, it's important to be sceptical and do your own research.

While selecting a food product for your pet, the focus should be on what's inside the can or bag, rather than on the famous face on it's packaging. It's advisable to check the labels, understand what the ingredients signify and consult with a vet or a pet nutrition expert when in doubt.

Celebrities frequently align themselves with products that are ethically produced or advocate for causes that are close to their hearts. As such, celebrity-endorsed dog food may advertise organic, non-GMO ingredients, sustainable farming practices, or cruelty-free testing. While these are all commendable traits, the celebrity endorsement shouldn't be the distinctive feature that decides your purchase.

Continuing on from this topic, emotional appeals are another powerful tactic used by advertisers in the pet industry. As we delve into this next advertising strategy, keep in mind that while celebrities may capture our interest, we owe it to our furry friends to critically evaluate the dog food options that are available to us.

Like many aspects of the modern, consumer-driven world, choosing the best product is often not as simple as accepting a recommendation at face value, even if that suggestion comes from a beloved celebrity. Celebrity-endorsed products should be evaluated like any other, with an emphasis on objective nutritional analysis, financial value, and above all, your dog's health and happiness.

Emotional Appeals are a strategic maneuver that many dog food companies use to entice consumers. It's a powerful tool that works by connecting with us at an emotional level. It's easy to feel our heartstrings tugged when we see a commercial featuring a happy, vigorous dog enjoying a meal, implicitly suggesting that buying their product will ensure our own dogs experience the same vitality and joy.

The effectiveness of these appeals lies in their ability to frame our buying decisions around our emotions rather than logical reasoning. We inherently value the well-being of our pets and want them to be happy, healthy, and energetic. Because of this, we are often drawn to products marketed with slogans like "Give your dog the life they deserve," or visually appealing imagery of dogs enjoying their meals.

Many dog food companies understand that consumers are not just purchasing a product; they are seeking ways to demonstrate love and care for their pets. Hence, advertisements evoke feelings of care, compassion, and concern for a dog's health and well-being. This emotional strategy creates a psychological bond between the consumer and the product, fostering brand loyalty.

An example of this is how some brands introduce narratives or stories into their advertisements. These narratives typically depict a dog's journey from being unwell, lethargic, or unhappy to regaining its zest for life after switching to the advertised brand's diet. The company's product is represented as the miracle cure that brought about the change. The underlying message? Feeding your beloved dog this brand of food will lead them to a happier, healthier life.

The use of such emotional appeals leaves a lasting impression on consumers and often influences their purchasing decisions. It's human nature to be moved by compelling stories and stirring emotions and the marketing specialists at dog food companies know this all too well.

Another common emotional appeal strategy involves the use of fear or guilt. For instance, some dog food commercials will emphasize the harm done by not choosing their brand. Advertisements might suggest that other dog foods could harm your pet's health and that you would be a neglectful owner if you choose them. This manipulative tactic leverages your love for your pet and your fear of causing them harm to sell their product.

Additionally, many dog food brands utilize the power of nostalgia. They align their products with the imagery of a simpler, idyllic past. This evokes in us a warm, comforting feeling and subtly suggests that by feeding our dogs their product, we are replicating the pure and natural essence of a bygone era when, presumably, dogs were healthier and happier.

These emotional appeals, when used effectively, can have a significant impact on the buyer's decisions. As knowledgeable dog owners, we must understand these tactics and be aware of their persuasive power. Recognising emotional appeals is the first step toward making informed, rational decisions about what is genuinely the best diet for our dogs. We must learn to separate the emotionally charged imagery and testimonials from the actual nutritional content and ingredients of the dog food.

Our love for our dogs is unchallengeable. However, it's crucial not to let that love cloud our judgment when it comes to selecting their diet. Instead of being swayed by emotional appeals, focus on understanding your dog's nutritional needs and the quality of ingredients used in the dog food you buy. In the end, the best indicator of a good dog food isn't how it makes us feel but how it keeps our dogs healthy and happy.

Decoding the Marketing Jargon

Having traversed the maze of celebrity endorsements and emotional appeals, it's now time to delve into the complex world of advertising language. The jargon used by dog food companies can often seem bewildering, but once we decode it, we can make more informed purchase decisions.

A common term you'll encounter is 'Complete and Balanced'. This phrase suggests that the product provides all the necessary nutrition your dog requires. To have its product labelled as 'complete and balanced', a dog food company must meet standards established by the Association of American Feed Control Officials (AAFCO). However, there is some criticism of these standards, primarily due to them being minimum requirements rather than optimum ones. Pet nutrition experts are largely in agreement that dogs require specific nutrients in specific quantities for them to thrive best.

'Natural' is another term you'll often see on dog food labels. According to AAFCO, 'natural' refers to any product free of artificial flavors, colors, or preservatives. The term seems appealing, but it doesn't necessarily mean the food is healthy. For example, a product could technically be labelled 'natural' even if it contains a large quantity of unhealthy or low-quality ingredients.

'Premium' and 'Gourmet' are words that suggest a higher quality product. It's important to note, however, that these terms are not regulated by any agency. This means companies have the freedom to use these words as they please, and they often do in order to lure in unsuspecting customers. Just because a food is labelled premium or gourmet does not mean it's superior in terms of nutrition or ingredient quality.

The phrase 'Grain-Free' is increasingly common these days. Many pet owners believe grains are bad for dogs, leading them to purchase grain-free foods. However, the truth is that most dogs can digest grains pretty well and can include them as part of a balanced diet. In fact, the FDA has linked certain grain-free diets to a heart disease called dilated cardiomyopathy (DCM) in dogs. As always, it's best to consult with your vet before making significant changes to your dog's diet.

Another term of interest is 'Human-Grade'. This refers to ingredients that are fit for human consumption. While this might sound appealing, keep in mind that humans and dogs have different nutritional requirements. So, although the ingredients are of a quality safe for human consumption, this does not mean the food offers the best nutrients for your dog.

'Holistic' is another term often seen on dog food labels. As with 'premium' and 'gourmet', this term is unregulated, and thus can be misleading. While the term itself refers to viewing and treating the body as an interconnected whole, when it is applied to dog food, it is likely simply a marketing tool.

Lastly, let's look at 'Meat Meal'. Contrary to popular belief, meat meal is not merely fillers or by-products. It is actually dehydrated and ground meat, and can contain high protein content. However, the specific type of animals used in the 'meal' and how they were raised can significantly affect its quality.

Understanding this jargon is an essential part of making informed decisions about what you feed your pet. Still, no matter how much we decode the language used in marketing, it should not replace the value of a good vet. If you have concerns or doubts about a particular brand or ingredient, don't hesitate to seek professional advice. Your pet's health always comes first.

Let us not forget the power we hold as consumers. Learning to navigate the complicated jargon isn't just about purchasing the right products; it's about advocating for clearer and more transparent language in pet food marketing. And with that, you're giving yourself the ability to make the best choices for your furry friend's diet.

Chapter 8:
The Natural Food Movement:
A Return to Old Ways?

In the aftermath of marketing strategies and dietary transitions, there's been a burgeoning interest in the natural food movement for dogs — an inclination towards raw or homemade meals suggestive of canine ancestral diets. This isn't without reason. Proponents argue such diets yield brighter coats, healthier skin, cleaner teeth, and higher energy levels. However, this isn't a one-size-fits-all solution. Critics warn of nutritional imbalances and the potential transmission of foodborne pathogens in raw diets. Homemade meals, while allowing for quality control, require significant time, effort, and knowledge to ensure all necessary nutrients are adequately provided. Furthermore, there is a lack of stringent regulations pertaining to raw or homemade canine diets, posing potential quality and safety risks. Therefore, it's essential to weigh the pros and cons, and consult with a veterinary nutritionist should you choose to tread this path. Whether deemed a return to old ways or a new dietary trend, the natural food movement undeniably raises an important question — what truly constitutes the best diet for our multifaceted furry companions?

Pros and Cons of Raw or Homemade Food

As responsible pet owners, we continuously search for the best practices to ensure our dogs' optimal health. One path that many are exploring is the incorporation of raw or homemade food into their pets' diets, which harks back to how our canine companions ate before commercial dog food dominated the scene.

The Advantages of Raw or Homemade Diets

There are numerous benefits to feeding our dogs raw or homemade meals. To start, offering raw or minimally processed food can provide our pets with a nutritionally balanced and varied diet, closer to what canines historically consumed. This balance is essential to support immune function, regulate weight, and promote overall health.

Feeding raw or homemade diets could potentially decrease the risk of dietary allergies and intolerances, which can cause a host of problems ranging from skin irritations to gastrointestinal issues. Often, these sensitivities are linked with the highly processed ingredients and artificial additives commonly found in commercial dog foods.

Another advantage of homemade diets is that they enable you to have complete control over what goes into your pet's bowl. Knowing each ingredient can be reassuring for pet owners, especially those who have dogs with specific dietary needs or allergies.

Raw diets, specifically, can benefit dogs' dental health. Chewing raw, meaty bones can help clean teeth and gums naturally, reducing the risk of dental disease.

Last but not least, many owners find that dogs simply enjoy homemade or raw meals more than kibble. The piqued interest and enthusiasm at meal times can be a reward in itself.

The Drawbacks of Raw or Homemade Diets

As with all decisions we make for our pets, it's also important to consider the potential disadvantages of raw or homemade diets. While there are significant gains, there also exist some challenges that need to be addressed.

Homemade diets can be time-consuming and expensive. Preparing a nutritionally balanced meal requires substantial effort, as you need to ensure that your pet's vitamin, mineral, and macronutrient needs are met. Acquiring high-quality raw ingredients can also come with a hefty price tag.

One of the biggest concerns when feeding dogs raw food is the risk of bacterial contamination, both for your pet and for your household. Raw meat can carry pathogens like Salmonella and E. Coli, which can cause serious illness in both animals and humans. Thus, meticulous handling and hygiene practices must be implemented.

Another challenge associated with homemade diets is the risk of nutrient imbalances. Even with the best intentions, it's easy to underestimate or overestimate your dog's nutritional needs if you aren't closely guided by a vet or a canine nutrition expert. Over time, deficiencies or excesses in certain nutrients can lead to health problems.

Finally, there are some dogs that might not adjust well to a raw or homemade diet. It's important to note that just like us, every dog has individual nutritional needs. Factors like age, breed, size, and health status can significantly influence how a dog responds to a particular diet.

In conclusion, the choice to feed your dog a raw or homemade diet is an individual one that should be made in close consultation with your vet or a canine nutrition expert. With careful preparation, strict sanitation procedures, and a commitment to trial and error, this feeding method can indeed offer a return to a more natural way of eating for our canine companions. However, it's always essential to weigh these benefits against the commitment that such a diet demands. Providing our dogs with the nutrition they need while also taking heed of their individual needs is, after all, the heart of responsible pet ownership.

Pet Food Regulations, Risks, and Safety

When it comes to feeding our furry companions, there's a lot more at stake than simply choosing between brands at a local pet store. Beyond the packaging and persuasive marketing, a deeper understanding of regulations, potential risks, and safety measures is necessary for responsible pet owners.

Navigating the world of pet food regulations can be a complex task. In the United States, the manufacture and distribution of pet foods are primarily regulated by the U.S. Food and Drug Administration (FDA), in compliance with the Federal Food, Drug, and Cosmetic Act (FFDCA). The regulations stipulate the safety and efficacy of the ingredients and labeling practices in pet food production.

FDA regulations also involve a level of cooperation with the Association of American Feed Control Officials (AAFCO), a voluntary membership association of local, state, and federal agencies responsible for regulating animal feed, including pet food. AAFCO does not carry regulatory authority but works to standardize labeling guidelines and provide ingredient definitions for pet food manufacturers.

The regulations seek to assure that pet foods, like human foods, are safe, properly produced, and accurately labeled. However, despite these regulations, there remain potential risks and critical safety considerations for pet owners.

Bacterial contamination is one of the most significant risks associated with both commercial and homemade pet foods. For instance, raw pet foods can carry harmful bacteria like Salmonella and E. Coli. Reports of bacterial outbreaks linked to commercial pet food are not uncommon, with some leading to product recalls. In 2020 alone, the FDA recalled over 20 different brands of dog food due to contamination with Salmonella, mold, and other foreign substances.

Moreover, commercially manufactured foods have also faced criticism for containing poorly labeled, potentially harmful ingredients. These include "meal" and "by-product" protein sources, artificial preservatives that may cause cancer, and chemical humectants that have been linked to toxic exposures and poisoning.

Stock contamination is another risk factor. Many types of commercial dog food contain rendered animal products, sourced from various locations. These products are processed under high heat, and potential contaminants such as heavy metals, pesticide residues, and even traces of the euthanasia drug pentobarbital have been found in some dog foods. As can be seen, despite regulations, certain risks continue to lurk.

Homemade foods, while allowing for more control over ingredients, pose challenges as well. Feeding dogs an unbalanced diet can lead to nutritional deficiencies or excesses, both of which can harm a dog's health. A study conducted by UC Davis revealed that 95% of homemade dog food recipes found online were nutritionally unbalanced.

Misinformation and lack of knowledge about dog nutrition can lead to misguided choices in homemade diets. Many owners are unaware that certain human foods, like onions, grapes, and chocolate, are toxic to dogs. Similarly, feeding dogs a diet that is too high in protein, fat, or carbohydrates can lead to health problems like obesity, heart disease, or pancreatitis.

The safety of your pet's food largely depends on proper storage, preparation, and handling practices. For example, raw food diets should be handled with the same caution as raw meat for human consumption to prevent bacterial contamination. All dishes and utensils should be washed and disinfected, and hands should be thoroughly washed before and after handling.

Commercially prepared foods should be stored in a cool, dry place and sealed to prevent contamination. For homemade diets, careful consideration should be given to ingredient sourcing, meal planning, and preparation to ensure nutritional completeness and balance. It's also recommended to consult a pet nutrition expert or a veterinarian before switching your dog to a homemade diet.

In conclusion, navigating the world of pet food regulations, risks, and safety is a crucial aspect of responsible pet ownership. Striving to learn more about these factors will ultimately enable you to make informed choices, ensuring the health, happiness, and longevity of your canine companions.

It's essential to remember that the overarching goal is to provide a diet that supports overall health and longevity for our furry friends. While the journey in selecting the right dog food might be a bit complex, it's definitely worth it for the unconditional love and companionship our dogs offer us.

Chapter 9:
Feeding Your Dog for Health and Longevity

In understanding the complexities of canine nutrition, it's clear that the journey from wolves to modern pets has brought about a seismic shift in how we feed our beloved pets. Like the transformation from raw, whole foods to commercial kibble, both innovations and compromises have been made. However, the key lies in arming ourselves with knowledge to make informed choices for our furry friends. It's crucial to remember that not all commercial food is bad, but we must discern the valuable nutrients from the questionable ingredients. Where possible, a balanced diet that harkens back to our pets' ancestral diet could be beneficial. Our journey through the history of dog food, the scientific make-up of a canine's nutritional needs, and the truths about kibble offers a stark reminder of the power we wield in determining the health and longevity of our pets. As we wrap up, let's carry with us these insights, always pushing for transparency from pet food manufacturers, questioning marketing tactics and advocating for healthier, more natural options. In doing so, we build a healthier life for our pets, one well-thought-out meal at a time.

Final Thoughts and Recommendations

I hope you've gained a deep understanding of how diet can directly impact the health and longevity of our beloved canine companions. As we have discovered, what goes into their bowls matters considerably. So, when selecting meals for your dogs, it is paramount that we critically evaluate our choices.

As a first step, always look for food with high-quality protein sources. Remember, dogs have descended from wolves and have similar dietary needs. So, whole meats or meat meals are great options. Foods labeled with generic terms like "meat" or "animal fats" should be avoided as they often indicate low-quality sources.

Next, avoid dog food with potentially harmful ingredients. While the list may be long, take note of a few important ones - preservatives like BHA and BHT, artificial colors and sweeteners, and generic by-products. Additionally, avoid foods with high grain content. While dogs are capable of digesting carbohydrates, their main diet should not be grains as they provide very little nutritional value.

Despite the criticisms leveled against commercial dog food, not all brands manufacture poor-quality food. There are many reputable companies producing nutritionally-balanced, wholesome dog food. It is these brands that dog owners should aim to trust and patronize. However, due diligence is necessary. Always read the label, know the ingredients, and research the brand.

Often, a mix of high-quality commercial food and home-cooked meals can prove beneficial. Raw or home-cooked food allows you greater control over the nutrients your dog gets. But, remember to consult a vet or a pet nutrition expert to ensure balance in nutrients. Inadequate or excess nutrients can lead to health complications.

Don't forget the importance of variety. Varying food can help provide a wider spectrum of nutrients and can make meals exciting for your pets. A diet with an assortment of proteins, fruits, vegetables, and minor amounts of grains can promote optimal health.

Portion control is equally essential regardless of whether it's commercial or home-cooked food. Obesity can lead to a plethora of health issues, including arthritis, heart disease, and diabetes. Hence, it's important to feed the right amount based on your dog's age, size, breed, and activity level.

One last thing that must not go unmentioned is the importance of regular vet check-ups. Even with a perfect diet, dogs can become susceptible to illnesses. Regular health screenings can help detect issues early and put intervention measures in place promptly.

Feeding dogs isn't about adhering to a one-size-fits-all rule. It's more about understanding the unique nutritional requirements of your dog and making the best choices based on that knowledge. There are dogs that live long, healthy lives on commercial dog food, whereas others might thrive on a raw diet. It's crucial to find what works best for your canine friend while keeping their health as the top priority.

It's worth spending time researching your dog's nutrition and consulting professionals when necessary. The right dietary choices could help your dog sidestep health troubles and live a longer, happier life.

In conclusion, remember that providing good nutrition is about holistic care for your dog – a combination of balanced diet, exercise, regular vet check-ups, and bundles of love. It is a profound responsibility, but one that comes with a worthwhile reward - a loyal friendship, days filled with play, and a happy wagging tail when you come home.

When it comes to feeding our dogs, it's easy to feel overwhelmed by the choices we need to make. But you're not alone. Many resources can help you understand your canine companion's nutritional requirements. Websites, books, vet consultations, and fellow pet owners can all provide valuable insights.

Knowing how influential diet is for our pets' health, wellness, and happiness, investing time into understanding dog nutrition is undoubtedly time well spent. The transformation that can happen in your dog's health from changes in their diet can be astonishing and fulfilling to any dog owner. After all, the ultimate goal is ensuring our four-legged family members are around, bringing joy to our lives, for as long as possible.

Resources for Further Exploration

Researching what's best to feed your canine companion is no small task. The world of dog nutrition can feel overwhelming and constantly evolving. However, just as we educate ourselves to make healthier eating choices, it's essential to do the same for our dogs. The following resources can help support further exploration into feeding your dog for health and longevity.

Websites and Blogs

DogFoodAdvisor - Pioneering in its scope, DogFoodAdvisor provides unbiased views on commercial dog food, breaking down ingredients, nutritional value, and recalls if any. It's a must-visit for any pet parent trying to make educated choices.

PetMD - A website with rich insights about pet health, including dog diets. This site is also useful for understanding potential health issues related to diet.

The Whole Dog Journal - An extensive blog that shares information about everything related to dogs including nutrition, behavior, and health.

Books

"The Royal Treatment" by Barbara Royal - This book discusses feeding pets from a holistic approach, emphasizing the benefits of natural diets.

"Feed Your Best Friend Better: Easy, Nutritional Meals and Treats for Dogs" by Rick Woodford - Offers practical advice and recipes to make homemade food for dogs.

Webinars and Online Courses

The Pet Food Institute - This institution offers webinars that explore nutrition science, industry trends, and regulatory updates about commercial pet food.

Coursera's Dog Emotion and Cognition: An offering from Duke University - While not directly about nutrition, understanding dog cognition can lend insight into their dietary needs.

Scientific Research

Refer to scholarly databases such as google scholar or JSTOR if you're interested in delving into scientific research about dog nutrition.

Remember, it's not just about feeding our dogs; it's about nurturing them and providing for their needs to the best of our abilities. As informed, caring guardians, the decisions we make around meal times can significantly impact their health and happiness, and ultimately, their lifespan. The resources above can help us make excellent choices as we navigate the journey of dog ownership. And in doing so, we not only foster a deeper bond with our beloved pets but are reciprocated with the joys of their vibrant health and vitality.